What Do Women Want?

What Do Women Want?

Self-Discovery Through Fantasy

Lucy Freeman

HUMAN SCIENCES PRESS
72 Fifth Avenue   3 Henrietta Street
NEW YORK, NY 10011 ● LONDON, WC2E 8LU

Library of Congress Catalog Number 77-28003

ISBN: 0-87705-298-0

Copyright © 1978 by Human Sciences Press
72 Fifth Avenue, New York, New York 10011

Printed in the United States of America
89   987654321

Library of Congress Cataloging in Publication Data

Freeman, Lucy.
  What do women want?

  Bibliography: p. 182
  Includes index.
  1. Women—Mental health.   2. Fantasy.   3. Self-perception.   I. Title.
RC451.4.W6F73   150'.19'52   77-28003
ISBN 0-87705-298-0

To Dale Schroedel
my niece
May she achieve what she truly wants.

CONTENTS

PREFACE

In recent years numerous books have appeared emphasizing the crippling influence of social customs and traditions on women. By comparison, there have been relatively few works describing women's struggles to attain emotional liberation—the liberation that comes from a deep knowledge of the self. I have chosen to focus this book on the classic psychoanalytic approach to the problems of women, since I believe emotional liberation can best be achieved through the framework with which Freud provided us.

After years of studying and writing about developments in the mental health field, and following the modifications and distortions of psychoanalytic theory and technique that regularly spring in and out of vogue, I am of the opinion that the traditional psychoanalytic approach provides the most meaningful way of viewing the self.

By stressing this form of self-understanding, I do not wish to negate the impact of society and culture on the thinking and behavior of women. However, the illusions of childhood, if left unexamined, sometimes persist into adulthood with tragic results. The fantasies that evolve from our two strongest drives—sexual and aggressive—may interfere with woman's fulfillment in many areas of her life, intensifying her emotional suffering.

Years spent in analysis have convinced me that sexual and aggressive fantasies, spun around unresolved conflicts, underlay my most troubled feelings. Some of these fantasies I was already vaguely aware of, others I denied vehemently at first. Only as I could accept their hidden influence on my life was I able to achieve what I think of as a certain peace of mind.

For the reader, I hope this book will encourage an introspective attitude, perhaps serve as a stepping off point for a deeper look at the self.

Lucy Freeman
New York, October 1977

FOREWORD

To most of the reading public, Lucy Freeman needs no introduction. Her career as a journalist at *The New York Times* was in itself a success story, followed by her best-selling book, *Fight Against Fears,* the story of her personal psychoanalysis. It has been followed by many other books dealing with various aspects of psychoanalysis. Some of these focus on clinical material, that is, case histories, such as *The Story of Anna O.,* which contained original research on Freud's first psychoanalytic case; *Celebrities on the Couch, Before I Kill More* and *Troubled Women.*

It is a pleasure for me to write a foreword to this volume which opens up a new field for Miss Freeman. In it she skillfully applies the insights gained over years to her focus on women and their internal struggle to achieve liberation via self-understanding. In a series of dramatic chapters, Miss Freeman guides the reader to greater levels of self-awareness and self-acceptance through the use of fantasy. She shows how fantasies provide a roadmap to what a woman wants and how they can be used constructively once properly understood.

Why is it so important to be aware of our fantasies? Because, much as dreams do, fantasies disclose the experiences which have formed our characters and are the sources of our behavior. The many ways in which fantasies represent our emotional and sexual lives are eloquently described by Miss Freeman. Fantasies portray our deepest wishes. They also define the nature of our relationship with those we love and admire or those we envy and hate. As children, our fantasies were efforts to "explain" the facts of life, including the genital differences, the nature of the sexual act and the eternal mystery of pregnancy and birth.

Our self-image and feelings of worth are detailed in our fantasy life. To the extent that a woman feels the lesser sex—dirty, dependent and incompetent—she sabotages her efforts to achieve liberation. True, the recent changes in socioeconomic and political attitudes toward the role of women represent dramatic strides, but without inner liberation, the newly acquired gains become severely limited. A woman can achieve far more than mere external changes if she becomes aware of the vital world within herself. It is this rich and revelatory inner world which remains unexplored in so many women today. How to gain access to this royal road to self-understanding is what Miss Freeman's book is all about.

Miss Freeman has moved from writing books which demonstrate the individual, specific value of analytic understanding to a new purpose: the metapsychological understanding of the role of fantasy.

She is to be congratulated on her success.

Walter A. Stewart, M.D.

November 26, 1977
New York

ACKNOWLEDGMENTS

My deep appreciation and thanks go to Norma Fox, editor-in-chief of Human Sciences Press, Inc., for helping to conceive and shape this book. My thanks also to Joanne Kass for her help with research and to Katherine Wolpe, Librarian, and Jeanette Taylor and Ruth M. Reynolds of the Library of the New York Psychoanalytic Institute.

Chapter 1

SUGAR AND SPICE—AND THINGS NOT SO NICE

Speaking once to Marie Bonaparte, Freud posed a beguiling challenge: "The great question that has never been answered and which I have not yet been able to answer, despite my thirty years of research into the feminine soul, is 'What does a woman want?' "

If women are asked what indeed they do want, most are likely to agree they want to love and be loved, to marry, raise children, and also have a career if they choose.

But how many women achieve all this? And why do so many fail?

Some women blame "society" for their failures. Others blame "men," who throughout the centuries have set the customs and laws discriminating against women. Man's long-standing hatred and enslavement of women

has been obvious. Today millions of women in far coun-
tries of the world are still treated as beasts of burden, and
are even sexually mutilated under the guise of "protection." (Young girls in some African and Asian tribes are
operated on before marriage to have their clitori removed and vaginas stitched so they will not be "tempted"
sexually; clitoral surgery was common in a few areas of
America as recently as the 1930's.)

"The history of civilization—primitive, ancient and
modern—is full of man's expression of his hostility and
envy of women," says Dr. Lawrence Friedman, psychoanalyst. Man envies woman's ability to give birth and
to have an unlimited number of orgasms, he explains.

"Woman is the lesser man," Tennyson wrote. She has
been set apart from man, considered slightly less than
human. In spite of the new freedoms, which actually
affect only a small percentage of the world's women,
many remain the target of hidden or open contempt from
the moment they are born—race, religion, color, or na-
tionality notwithstanding. They are accused of being by
nature stupid, naive, inept, anxious, contentious, hysterical, and indecisive. Woman is still frequently called "the
weaker sex."

Poets and philosophers have long spoken unkindly of
women. Menander wrote, "A woman is necessarily an
evil." Horace claimed, "A fickle and changeful thing is
woman ever." Later, Pope held that "every woman is at
heart a rake," and Schopenhauer claimed, "Dissimulation
is innate in woman." Shakespeare's "Frailty, thy name is
Woman!" is perhaps the most famous literary put-down of
the female sex.

The woman of today has come a long way in achieving equality with men. Now perhaps she can afford to face
some of the conflicts within herself that may have con-

tributed to her unhappiness. She can still blame society, and men, for real, ongoing injustices—but not for an inner sense of despair or for repressed anger that has nothing to do with external reality.

One way a woman may understand why she has not yet achieved what she wants is to examine her fantasies. Fantasies reveal our deepest desires, mirroring wishes that have little or nothing to do with reality—wishes that are the key to our most intense conflicts. Fantasies furnish important clues to understanding who we are. They portray what psychoanalysts call the "idealized self" but, more important, the "unidealized self." They may keep a woman from achieving what she consciously wants.

A single woman, who has turned down marriage proposals from man after man, insists defiantly, "But I really *want* to get married." She does not realize her unconscious wishes keep her from accepting an eligible man. The wishes that hold back a woman from happiness are usually hidden from her awareness and thus seem unreal to her even though they may be more powerful than the wishes of which she is aware.

A fantasy may be thought of as the visualization of a wish (the Greek *phantasia* means "a making visible"). We may fantasize what we dare not do (murder a parent) or what we dare do (become rich and famous). Our fantasies exist both in the unconscious part of the mind, which does its own free thinking, uncensored by the conscious, and in the conscious part of our mind, where our fantasies are controlled.

Fantasies appear in our daydreams and in our dreams at night. Those in daydreams are conscious, those in night dreams, unconscious. The fantasy in a daydream usually masks an unconscious fantasy forbidden or dangerous to our self-esteem. That forbidden or dangerous fantasy originated in childhood but remains as powerful as when it first came to mind, for the unconscious is timeless—no wish ever disappears.

Everyone has fantasies, using them to escape from what is often harsh reality. Freud described a fantasy as "the fulfillment of a wish, or a correction of unsatisfying reality." We need fantasies, for many of our deepest childhood wishes can never be gratified in reality and so we turn occasionally to our fantasies and dreams for their fulfillment.

In providing a momentary escape from real life, fantasy helps us endure it with more grace, dignity, and humor than we might otherwise muster. Fantasy gives us a sense of independence. We need nobody, nothing. We depend only on our imagination to fulfill our wishes. In fantasy the rich and the poor are equal. In fantasy everyone can concoct the most exotic and erotic of love scenes, or the bloodiest of revenges.

An unconscious fantasy usually distorts reality, for it was formed when we were children and our ability to reason was undeveloped. We tried as best we could to explain to ourselves the mysteries of an expanding, fascinating, but sometimes terrifying world. We had to cope not only with our own distortions of reality, but with those of our parents, not daring to defy them if we thought them wrong, for fear they would no longer love us and we would perish.

Each current conscious fantasy is linked to a past unconscious one. The current fantasy stimulates thoughts of some desire which has caused us conflict in the past. A single recurring fantasy thus threads through our lives—with more or less variation—from our earliest days to the present.

All fantasies, even those in daydreams, spring from our unconscious, which is savage, primitive, psychotic-like. This part of our mind brooks no compromise, heeds no reason. Once in a while, in spite of our vigilance, an irrational thought escapes in a slip of the tongue.

A married woman, while playing bridge, rose from the table and said apologetically to her three companions, "Excuse me. I have to go kill my husband." She meant to say "call." There was a roar of laughter at the slip, which revealed her unconscious wish to get rid of a tyrannical husband, one to whom she had to report even from the bridge table.

The forgetting of a name or of an appointment also reveals unconscious wishes. We do not want to do things that cause us pain, or that we anticipate will bring pain; our unconscious, always bent on pleasure, may take over when we act against our deeper wishes. One woman, on her way to a dinner party given by someone she disliked and whose company she usually avoided, forgot her hostess's address. She had to return by taxi to her apartment, miles away, to look up the unlisted telephone number, call, and get the correct address. She arrived late to face a furious hostess. Furious at herself as well, she realized she had not wanted to go in the first place. Her unconscious had tried to prevent her from giving in to a painful experience.

In a sense, we live in two worlds. One is the world in which we communicate with others, the external world of work and play. The second is the world in which our secret wishes reign. Our reason, or conscious thought, dominates the world of outer reality. Our unconscious, or primitive thought, rules the world of inner reality.

Our unconscious has faith in the magic of a wish—to wish for something is to get it. The wish is very important to our lives. It is the way we survive. We are governed by our wishes—we cannot do anything without first wishing it. To get up in the morning, we must wish to rise. The wish propels us into the day, into living. But often our wishes are not simple. If carried out, they would shame us or perhaps bring a disgraceful punishment, even death. Therefore we must censor our wishes, deciding which are desirable to act on and which are not. Sometimes a wish we consider evil is banished so swiftly we are scarcely aware of it.

Fantasy is the psychic counterpart of a physical impulse that is repressed. Like a safety valve, fantasy provides an outlet for a repressed wish. In daydreams the wish appears in very disguised form, while in our dreams at night it is more thinly disguised. Our dangerous wishes stem from our love and hate impulses—the two strongest urges we possess.

A fantasy gives the temporary illusion our desire has been fulfilled. It makes the impossible possible—for a moment, real. And it protects us in that the greater danger would have been to act upon the wish, not merely to fantasize about it.

Fantasy has other uses. Our daydreams, our conscious fantasies, enhance our self-esteem, help us maintain the image of ourselves as noble, gallant, lovable human beings who deserve the best of everything. Fantasies ease loneliness. Children, when they are left alone, will talk to animals, fantasizing them as human. Or they act out in their play some trauma of their lives, thereby diminishing the anxiety connected with it.

Daydreams may also lead to creativity. One woman may use her fantasies to paint, another to design a skyscraper, a third to compose a concerto, a fourth to write a movie script.

Ancient man, like children, used fantasy to decrease his terror of the unknown. To ease his fear of lightning, he imagined it to be a thunderbolt thrown by a wrathful god. He considered the sun a beneficent god driving a chariot across the heavens. A flood or earthquake he believed caused by gods who were angry, who could be appeased only by prayer, atonement, and sacrifice. Ancient man had not yet developed enough intelligence to understand the wonders of nature scientifically or to realize his "gods" were images of his parents.

Throughout the ages fantasies have helped mankind survive the terrors, frustrations, and pains of living. Even the so-called normal woman, who leads a comparatively conventional life, falls in love, marries, has children and takes care of them lovingly, harbors many compelling, opposing wishes in her unconscious. The very process of becoming civilized, of having to control many of our strongest impulses, creates conflicts and fantasies.

If a woman has not achieved what she says she wants, she stands a far better chance of getting it if she can become aware of some of her hidden fantasies via their link to the conscious fantasies. She may pay a high psychic price if she lives too intensely in the alluring world of fantasy, if her secret wishes play too powerful a role in her life, overwhelming her conscious desires.

Fantasies can chain her to impossible childhood dreams rather than help free her for mature achievements. Engaging in indiscriminate sexual affairs, for instance, shows that a woman is still under the spell of childhood fantasies. Wishing to imitate a Don Juan's casual approach to sex is not the same as becoming equal to a man in genuine sexual freedom. Or of achieving true femininity.

For a woman to be able to make the important decisions of her life wisely, she must feel emotionally free. This means being aware of such deeper feelings as fear, hatred, dependency. If she denies these feelings she thwarts her own emotional liberation and is apt to remain in a rigid mental bind all her life.

True self-esteem for a woman includes acknowledging that she possesses every human feeling. To achieve this self-esteem many women need to recognize more fully the large part their fantasies play in preventing their emotional liberation.

Possibly our most important freedom is emotional freedom—the freedom to act as we wisely choose, taking into account the limitations imposed by society. This is far different from being driven into obsessive behavior that is destructive to ourselves and others.

Promiscuity, alcoholism, obesity, depression—these show the still-powerful influence of self-defeating fantasies never accepted by a woman as part of childhood thinking. The function and importance of fantasy apply also to men. But certain "polar" fantasies—lifelong, persistent wishes—appear more commonly in women, while others are unique to women, and these fantasies are described in the following pages.

Chapter 2

AND THEY LIVED HAPPILY EVER AFTER

Many women sit around waiting for the illusionary Mr. Right. They fantasize that as soon as he magically appears, their lives will change, all their romantic and sexual desires will be fulfilled.

A newspaper reporter, thirty-three years old, sits at her desk in a large city room, surrounded by other reporters, their typewriters clicking, their voices buzzing as they gather the day's news. She is lost in reverie thinking of the movie she saw the night before in which Jack Nicholson plays a detective. She is desperately in love with Nicholson, even though he appeared throughout half the film with his nose smashed, bloody, and stitched. She adores his lean, somewhat cruel but sensual face, his seductive, mocking voice. She believes that if she met him, they would fall in love, marry, and live happily ever after.

Ten blocks away, in a midtown Manhattan brokerage office, a woman of forty-three, divorced, with two children in college, has the same daydream about Robert Redford. His photographs adorn the walls of her bedroom. His face is the last thing she sees at night, the first in the morning. She haunts movie houses that run his old films. She imagines herself sleeping close to him all night, as Barbra Streisand did in "The Way We Were." She wishes she could live with him the rest of her life, that he would divorce his wife and marry her.

The world is full of women yearning for the absent Prince Charming. He may be Sinatra, Nureyev, Baryshnikov, or Namath—anyone of heroic stature. And, most important, ineligible.

Though she dreams of her Prince Charming falling in love with her, the woman knows in her heart he never will, that she will never even meet him, much less hold him in her arms. This does not matter—what does is that he offers an outlet for her repressed feelings of idolatrous love. It is not so much who he *is* but who he *represents* that counts. He stands for an early, passionate love in her life—her first love.

The woman who yearns constantly for the unattainable knight in shining armor, who clings to an elusive man as her way of expressing love, is telling the world she does not want a real man. She is caught up in the illusion of love. Girlish, adolescent love for the adored man in her life—her father. She has carried the torch into adulthood. Her familial attachment prevents her from entering into any relationship with a man that may be intimate and enduring, for she never really looks at a man as a human being but as the reflected idol of her youth. Such a woman still believes in one of the most entrenched fantasies of girlhood—the Cinderella story, in which Prince Charming rescues the unfortunate girl from her life of drudgery and despair and lives happily ever after with her.

Why does this famous fairy tale exert such a powerful effect on the fantasy lives of women? Because it expresses so many of their wishes as little girls. Since the little girl thinks of herself as a waif, a slave to her mean, harsh mother, her most intense desire is that a strong, handsome man will sweep her off her feet and save her from a life of poverty, starvation, and cruel treatment.

These are the *conscious* wishes expressed in the story of Cinderella. But what are the *unconscious* ones to which they are linked? First and foremost, the story fulfills the little girl's wish to marry her own father. In her unconscious, the heroic Prince Charming represents her father, whose protection and beneficence she craves. The wicked stepmother represents her real mother—her rival for her father's love and the source of all the frustration and deprivation she has felt since the day she was born. The selfish stepsisters in the story stand for the little girl's siblings, whom she wishes had never been born (if she were the only child she would get all her mother's love).

The Cinderella story also reveals the girl's wish that she had been born a boy. The Fairy Godmother's magic "wand" represents the powerful penis, possessing the ability to create a fancy carriage and a coachman out of a pumpkin—but only until midnight (an erection can last only so long). The wish to be a boy is fulfilled symbolically when the Prince fits the glass slipper on Cinderella's tiny foot, adding a fancy adornment (the phallus) to her small "appendage."

While the purpose of fairy tales such as Cinderella appears primarily as entertainment, they also serve the important function of fulfilling in fantasy both the conscious and unconscious sexual and aggressive drives. Fairy tales speak of love and of hate. Children need at times to win out over the terrifying "giants" to whom they must submit (their parents). They actually lose most of the battles of the nursery, but they can win them in fantasy as

they listen to fairy tales in which the "little people"—
elves, leprechauns, animals, or insects—behead menacing
giants, kill the big bad wolf, or burn the wicked witch
alive.

Often both the "good" and the "bad" side of a parent
appear. The "good" parent is the rescuer, the "bad," the
villain who pursues the child. The "bad" mother becomes
the wicked witch, whose broomstick, usually placed between her legs as she rides it, is equated with a hidden
penis. Dr. Franz Ricklin, psychoanalyst, notes the almost
inevitable presence in fairy tales of the cruel stepmother,
as well as the sexual pursuit of the daughter by the father.

Psychoanalysts have long compared the sexual symbolism in fairy tales to that of dreams. Dr. Ben Rubenstein
points out that the least disguised wish in the Cinderella
story is the resolution of her sexual rivalry with her
mother, symbolized by the stepmother. He says that the
identification of little girls with "poor, mistreated, dirty
Cinderella portrays the reversal of the sadistic, punitive
feelings they experience in relationship to the mother and
siblings." The little girls turn their angry feelings on
themselves, as Cinderella does, and become the "drudge
of all work", allowing them to triumph over the guilt at
their sadistic wishes. In Grimm's version, Cinderella gets
revenge on her greedy stepsisters by ordering doves to
pluck out their eyes, thus revealing at last her original
hatred of them.

Fairy tales play an important part in the child's struggle to cope with a difficult real-life environment and aid
in the understanding and control of sexual and aggressive
wishes. They reassure the child that he or she can overcome the terrifying obstacles that might beset them on
the way to falling in love and getting married. The little
girl "obtains a fulfillment in imagination of those unconscious wishes which she cannot yet obtain in reality,"

maintains Dr. Géza Róheim, as he points out that all fairy tales have a happy ending. Until recently, most Hollywood movies were like fairy tales, ending with the man and woman getting married, never facing the disillusionment that was bound to come.

Along with the story of Cinderella, little girls are perhaps most influenced by the tales of the Sleeping Beauty and Beauty and the Beast.

In the latter, a wealthy father with three daughters asks what gifts they wish him to bring back from a journey. The two older sisters want jewels, but the youngest, Beauty, requests only a rose. During his trip, the father loses his fortune but stops to steal a rose for Beauty when he comes upon a garden owned by a Beast. The Beast sees him steal the rose, and threatens to kill him. The father promises the Beast his youngest daughter if he will spare his life. When Beauty meets the Beast, she is horrified by his ugliness. But she keeps her father's bargain and goes to the Beast's castle, even as she insists she will never marry him. One day, in desperation, she leaves him. Eventually however she decides to return, and finds him near death, pining for her. She then agrees to marry the Beast, whereupon he is transformed into a handsome prince.

According to Dr. Jacques Barchilon, this fairy tale presents as a romantic love story what the virgin girl fears as brutal conquest—the act of sex. The "beastly" character of the Prince symbolizes the unconscious taboo against incest. To a little girl the idea of sexually loving her father is "monstrous." The sexual aspect of a daughter's love for her father is, however, a psychic reality, and it is the little girl's task to eventually transfer her love for her father to a more appropriate male. In one way she is prepared for this by hearing the story of Beauty and the Beast, in which she is reassured that the Beast is really "kind" and will not hurt her, that even though he wishes to conquer her sexually, he is willing to wait for her to make up her mind so his eventual conquest will be less terrifying. He is both the father figure and the prospective husband, according to Barchilon. The Beast-Prince is "a symbol announcing sexual conquest but this conquest must be made acceptable to the child. She has lost the father she loves by going to live with the Beast. She expects to die every day, that is, face sexuality personified in the Beast."

Discussing the meaning of the rose in the story, Dr. Thomas Mintz points out it is the picking of a *rose* from his garden that so enrages the Beast. "Why is the rose the specific flower mentioned? Why not just any flower?" asks Mintz.

He says the rose stands for "the beginnings of female sexuality in the woman ... these female sexual stirrings may be thought of as being the onset of menses (the first rose that is plucked from the garden—the womb) or as the onset of intercourse or thoughts thereof (defloration)." The red of the rose symbolizes the blood which issues from a young woman's body during menstruation and after her first sexual act, which frightens her, but which in this fairy tale is transformed into something beautiful, fragrant, and desirable. As soon as Beauty agrees to marry the Beast, he is changed into a Prince, just as "love transforms what is ugly, such as a penis, sexuality, animal passion into what is beautiful."

In the tale of Sleeping Beauty, the traditional theme of "waiting for the right man" corresponds with the fantasies of many young girls. Yet why do so many adult women still cling to the illusion that they will fall in love with a Prince Charming? Why are they unable to distinguish between the demands of reality and the storybook world? Because they have not successfully worked through their Oedipal feelings for their father. While such feelings are entirely natural to all little girls, forming an important psychosexual stage through which they must pass in order to be able later to love an appropriate man, they signal immaturity in grown women. Such women have been unable to transfer their love for their father to a man outside the family. In a general sense, psychoanalysts tell us this is due to a lack of emotional security in childhood. The experiences they went through with their mothers and fathers did not give them enough of a sense of trust and self-confidence to permit them to progress to a more mature stage, one in which they no longer need the illusion of romantic love.

If a woman has been unable to change her earlier romantic concept of love to a more realistic one, she may never stop searching for a Prince Charming. She may never know the difference between love as fairy tales portray it and the love that develops between two adults who are able and willing to accept reality. The happiness of fairy tales is not the happiness of the mature woman but of the little girl who had the fantasy marriage would make up for all her childhood frustrations, take care of her childhood longings, and erase all the emotional scars of childhood.

There is a danger, if a woman lives too intensely in the fairy tale world of childhood, that she will not adjust to the harsher demands of the real world. One woman of thirty-five, who had experienced two unhappy marriages, told her psychoanalyst, "I expected marriage to solve all my problems. To give me a freedom and joy I had never known. Instead I discovered I had put a leash around my neck, dragged around at the whim of my husband. Marriage was not a sharing, but an exploitation. I felt a slave, just like my mother had been to my father."

Another unhappily married woman told her analyst, "The night I got married, I dreamed I was in a graveyard, standing on a tombstone." To her, marriage and death were synonymous. Her father had left her mother when she was eight and, in her fantasy, to marry meant she would slowly wither away and die, as her mother had done.

Many a woman has swiftly become disillusioned with marriage—a sad ending to her fairy tale expectations. True, she may have expected too much from marriage in the first place and true, she may have chosen a man with whom no woman could live. But essentially, such a woman has been the victim of fantasies, powerful since childhood, that have interfered with her capacity to build a close relationship with a man. She is incapable as yet of mature love.

What is mature love? It is the result of a complicated feeling that has evolved through many stages from the day we were born. It encompasses not only passionate sensual love, but a love founded on friendship and trust, a love emanating from respect and admiration, a love that contains in it the wish to share and comfort and help.

As babies we knew only self-love. Then we learned to love another person—first our mothers, then our fathers. There comes a stage at which we love someone of the same sex, someone like ourselves. Finally, we feel love for someone of the opposite sex. Each stage has its own fantasies, which combine and overlap with fantasies of both previous and successive stages.

Mature love is a love that lasts, as opposed to the temporary display of passion known as "being in love," or "falling madly in love." Freud compared the latter to a psychotic state in which the love object is overidealized, seen as "perfect." As Helene Deutsch puts it, many women know the feeling of "being in love" but not "love." They experience love only as an "uncritically overestimating ecstasy of feeling that has nothing to do with the real value of the object . . . As soon as the ecstasy has passed, the love disappears. What remains is indifference or hatred with regard to the man so ardently loved before."

All the negative feelings and anxieties previously hidden, suppressed by the ecstasy, now come to the fore and "only the seamy side of the relationship is recalled." Closer examination shows, according to Deutsch, the woman "loved only a phantom, a fictitious ideal to which she temporarily gave a real name. After a shorter or longer period she experiences the same love enthusiasm for another phantom, and this will suffer the same fate." The woman's own need to be "*in* love" gives her the illusion of loving.

The woman's fantasy that the man is her father—at first the "good," then the "bad" father—is the "unconscious determinant of the love relationship that leads to the illusion of love," Deutsch maintains. All awareness of the father's "badness" is suppressed until after her sexual desire has been satisfied.

An unsatisfactory split occurs in many women between their sexuality and the erotic longing for a love ideal, as all their lives they yearn for a *grande passion,* even though they may be married and sexually satisfied. They are caught in what Deutsch calls "the adolescent split between eroticism and sexuality." She describes one of the goals of a mature woman as "the ability gradually to shape the erotic longing in such a way that it does not negate the direct experience of sexuality, or does not impose too severe erotic conditions."

The "happily ever after" image comes in part from the girl's attachment to her father. In the long run, as Freud's biographer Ernest Jones warned, a girl must choose between "sacrificing her erotic attachment to her father and sacrificing her femininity." She must renounce either her "incest" or her "sex." If she spends the rest of her life "in love" with her father, whether she has sex with hundreds of men, or with none, she has little chance of getting close to any one man.

The best marriages, according to psychoanalysts, are built on attachments that are not conflicted, where the woman feels little anger at the man. A woman's ability to tolerate imperfections in the man, and his ability to accept her faults, is the important factor in a happy marriage.

In the eyes of Dr. Sandor Rado, so-called "romantic love" is made up of sexual attraction and need, a relapse to the dependent state of childhood, which offers emotional security of a very infantile kind, and self-love. Rado maintains, "When one individual finds the person who triggers and integrates these three emotional forces in himself, he is going to have an explosive experience. Sexual intercourse in the being in love state is obviously an experience much superior to a sexual experience outside of the being in love state. All our drama and fiction for the last two thousand years has revolved around the problem of romantic love and of executing this love in the sex act."

Our psyches try, always, to get rid of whatever causes pain and to retain whatever is a source of pleasure. When someone is a source of genital pleasure (the strongest kind of pleasure one person can give another), the relationship is usually of the "being in love" type. This explains why so many women choose to remain with men who beat them, or who are cruel to them in other ways, but who give them sexual pleasure. They endure the sadism in order to get the occasional genital "explosive experience," in Rado's words. These women are sacrificing the chance for a far more stable, though perhaps less violently exciting, relationship with a man who could be tender and loving.

The feeling of love does not spring full-blown when we reach adolescence. It starts at birth, perhaps even pre-natally. A baby girl's first feeling of love is for her mother. She experiences the feeling of security as she is kissed, held close, and taken care of. As she grows, the little girl becomes more independent, her security resting more with her own acts and thoughts. Yet her yearning for the earlier type of security felt with her mother always remains to some degree; she will especially yearn for it in times of stress.

A woman who falls "madly in love" believes the man will be in the same relationship to her as her mother used to be. She is seeking an infantile dependence on the man, using him as a mother substitute. The illusion of having recaptured that early security masks for the moment any objective feelings she may have about herself or the man. She feels only, "If I have you, darling, the rest of the world doesn't matter. I don't care what happens tomorrow." She yearns only for him to hold her close, to merge with him, to have him possess her completely, as she wishes to possess him. She is insanely jealous of all other women he may find attractive.

A little girl has every right to feel secure in her mother's love. But as a woman, she cannot expect a man to take care of her in the same sense her mother did. Most of the emotional needs of an adult are of such a nature that another person can never satisfy them. They can be fulfilled only by our own efforts. To the extent a woman is gripped by "in love" feelings, she renounces her status as an adult. She behaves like a baby relying on her mother to take care of her. The result is a crippling of her personality. She cannot be both fully mature and "madly in love" at the same time—one negates the other.

The greater a woman's insecurity, due to emotional needs unmet when she was still a girl, the greater may be her desire to propel herself into the "in love" state. She seeks to satisfy her earlier need for love by finding a man who appears strong and protective, but who is equally insecure within. The more self-esteem she possesses, the less capable will she be of falling "madly in love," and the less inclined to give up her self-sufficiency and independence. Instead of overidealizing a man, she will see him as human, with faults, accept him as he is, respect and admire his good qualities, and seek a satisfactory if not eternally passionate sex life with him.

It is paradoxical that the woman most in need of emotional security from a man will choose the man least likely to give it to her, while the woman least in need of it will select the man most capable of giving it. As one woman of thirty-five remarked plaintively to her psychoanalyst, "If Grand Central Station were filled door to door with ten thousand emotionally mature men, and one emotional cripple, I would head unerringly for the one emotional cripple."

Why is the wish to believe the loved one "perfect" so strong in us? According to Dr. Robert C. Bak, this overidealization masks an underlying hatred which, for the moment, lies dormant . We all hide within us hostile impulses which we sense but which we do not wish to display until we have secured the loved one's vow of undying adoration—and, usually, possession of his body as well. As soon as the man becomes in any way frustrating or rejecting, our hatred rises to the surface. We then denigrate, devalue, perhaps even wish to destroy him. When disillusionment is very strong, suicide or murder may take place.

Bak also theorizes that the "in love" state, as compared to mature love, is an attempt to restore the lost, beloved mother of childhood. The woman who goes from man to man is seeking to replace the love of her mother, a love that comforts and warms. She engages in one love affair after another out of what Bak calls "the intensity of her own emotion" rather than any interest in the man as a mate.

In describing the "in love" state as based on undoing the separation of mother and child, as well as all later separations and losses of loved ones, Bak concludes: "It would seem that early loss or deprivation, incomplete separation, and/or prolonged clinging promote fusion with the object and thus create a difficulty in the transition from 'in love' to loving."

We may think of such love, in a sense, as sexualized mourning, in contrast to the more adult feeling of love without excessive sorrow, anger, or guilt (anger, then guilt at the angry feelings, are always part of the mourning process).

Moreover, when a woman has not given up her childish dependent need for her mother—which means too she has never worked through her deep attachment for her father—whatever man she is "in love" with represents her father and will thus cause her to feel guilty, as though she is taking her father from her mother. She experiences the feeling of "guilty triumph," in Bak's words, and she will seek the same fate she wished for her mother—to be cast out—as punishment for her guilt.

One divorced woman told her psychoanalyst she feared she would end up as her mother did—old, alone, without a husband.

"Like mother, like daughter," she said grimly.

"You don't have to follow in your mother's footsteps if you will face the guilt you felt when your father left her to marry another woman," the psychoanalyst said.

"I felt very sorry for my mother, but not guilty," she protested.

"You felt sorry but you also felt a sense of triumph

because another woman took your father from your mother, as you wished to do."

At first she was outraged at this suggestion, then realized it was true. She had hidden from herself all feelings of "guilty triumph." This had led to her belief she deserved the same fate as her mother.

"Love is no simple thing, like in the storybooks, is it?" she said to the psychoanalyst.

"Love is a very complicated emotion," he replied.

"Why?" she asked.

"Because it depends on so many of the experiences we have undergone as children with our mother and father," he said. "A child who sees little but hate in the household can hardly be expected to know how to love in any mature sense. His cry for love will always be on an infantile level."

Fairy tale love is fine for little girls. It fulfills their needs early in their lives. But if, as women, they still live enthralled by the myth of Prince Charming and fail to connect the wish for a handsome hero to their earliest desire for their father's love, their emotional liberation will suffer.

Chapter 3

LET THE PUNISHMENT FIT THE "CRIME"

The innocent fantasies revealed in fairy tales are closely connected to the sexual fantasies of women. They form part of the same web of illusion women spin to protect themselves from the shameful, embarrassing truth that they are still in love with and sexually desire their fathers. This love is natural for every little girl, and prepares her to feel love later in life. She is in emotional trouble only when she is unable to go beyond it, never giving up her father as the sole object of her love.

Because a grown woman feels such love as obscene, taboo, she conjures up fantasies in which another man is the target of her sensual urges. One woman, for instance, imagines she is only ten years old, brought to the court of a famous king by her poor, starving mother who says to her, "If you please the King, he'll give us money and we can buy food and clothes."

Her mother and she enter the palace and are taken before the King. Sitting high on a throne, he orders the mother to leave. The mother whispers to the little girl, "Remember—let him do anything he wants. Perform well!"

The little girl, feeling honored to be in the presence of such a great man, waits for him to tell her what to do. The King dismisses all his attendants. He and the little girl are left alone in the huge, elegantly decorated room. "Come sit on my lap," he says to her.

She walks over to him, excited to be allowed near this powerful man and thrilled by his muscular physique. The King pulls up his robe and shows her his naked body. He takes her on his lap and slowly, gently, inserts his large penis into her small vagina. At first this hurts, but the little girl feels it as a welcome hurt which changes into a mounting sexual desire. Hearing her mother say, "Perform well!", she reaches a sexual climax—her first orgasm. The King, too, shakes in frenzied orgasm as he pours his semen all over her, for her tiny vagina is too small to hold much of it.

This is the fantasy of a thirty-year-old woman, an actress, who has been married for eight years to an advertising executive with whom she has sex once or twice a month. Sometimes she uses the fantasy to masturbate at night when he is asleep and she feels sexually aroused. She is not seeking a divorce since she is not in love with another man and both likes and respects her husband—though she is unable to understand why he is not more sexually active. As far as she knows, he does not have sex with any other woman; he appears to be a man without a strong sexual drive.

Many women have sexual fantasies in order to reach orgasm as they masturbate, or while in the act of sex with a lover or husband. Are such fantasies "right" or "wrong," "helpful" or "harmful"?

There is no "right" or "wrong" to a fantasy, according to psychoanalysts. A fantasy *is*. It serves some purpose in our psyche, usually a protective one, disguising from us our deep, frustrated wishes.

A fantasy remains in the unconscious part of our minds, where there is no concept of time such as we know it in our rational lives. "There is nothing in the Id that corresponds to the idea of time; there is no recognition of the passage of time, and—a thing that is most remarkable and awaits consideration in philosophical thought—no alteration in its mental processes produced by the passage of time," says Freud. "Wishful impulses which have never passed beyond the Id, but impressions, too, which have been sunk into the Id by repression, are virtually immortal; after the passage of decades they behave as if they had just occurred."

Of our "wishful impulses," the two strongest are our sexual and aggressive urges. We must never underestimate the strength of either. Such urges are clear in the fantasies accompanying our psychosexual development. The fantasies stem from our own natural passions and our early experiences with our mother, father, and siblings. The consciously erotic fantasies of adulthood mirror the early erotic fantasies of childhood, but at a more genital level. Prince Charming is transformed into a seducer, a lecher, a rapist. Idealistic romance is overwhelmed by a sexual passion so strong that it must be denied as originating in the self. Blame is placed instead on the older woman—the mother (the "madam" who pushes the younger girl into sexual acts), or the older man—the father (the pimp or rapist).

In the actress's fantasy, previously described, her mother insists the little girl subject herself to the sexual advances of the King. He symbolizes the father of her childhood, whom she adored as a little girl. There are probably many mothers who unconsciously urge their daughters to "be nice to Daddy" so he will not leave home, will not fail to provide food and shelter. The actress is saying, in her fantasy, that she sees her mother as deliberately throwing her into her father's arms—which plays into her own wish to take him away from her mother.

In the four main stages of a girl's psychosexual development—oral, anal, phallic, and genital—typical fantasies accompany each stage. The original erotic love of the self is accompanied by masturbatory fantasies. Erotic love of someone of the same sex, such as mother, sister, or grandmother, brings with it lesbian fantasies. Finally, erotic love of a member of the opposite sex is expressed through heterosexual fantasies.

One woman of twenty-eight, describing a sexual fantasy to her analyst, said: "While I'm having sex with my husband, I have the fantasy I am eleven years old. The man is much older, a stranger I have picked up on a train. He seduces me in the privacy of a compartment. He lays me down on the bed and slowly undresses me and then fondles and caresses, with his lips, my whole body, until I am aroused. Then he gets on top of me, puts his penis inside me, and I come. This fantasy always works. Without it, I don't achieve an orgasm."

"Why, in your fantasy, are you eleven years old?" asked the analyst.

"I don't know," she answered.

"Do you remember anything happening, in a sexual sense, when you were eleven?"

She thought for a moment, then said, "I think that was about the time my best girl friend and I would go in back of our garage, where we would be hidden by bushes, and mutually masturbate each other."

"Was that your first introduction to sexual activity with another person?"

"Yes."

"So you must have had sexual fantasies centering on that experience," the analyst said.

"You mean it is not an accident that now, in my fantasies, I choose the age of eleven?" she asked.

"Nothing in a fantasy is an accident," he replied. "Usually it relates to some experience in your childhood. You probably imagined your friend was a man, arousing you to orgasm. Or that you were the man, your finger substituting for the penis, when you aroused her. In your fantasy, you play both roles, as one always does in a fantasy."

This woman, an only child, had grown up feeling very lonely because both parents were always busy with their own activities. She remembered further that the sexual experience with her friend happened just after she learned her father was sexually involved with the wife of a close business associate. In a way, by using her fantasy of a sexual encounter with an older man to achieve orgasm while having intercourse with her own husband, she was identifying with and imitating her father's adulterous behavior.

Another woman said to her analyst, "I never need to have fantasies when I first meet a man. Then the feeling of sudden, spontaneous passion, of desperate craving for him is enough to carry me to orgasm. But as I become disillusioned with the man, for one reason or another—maybe he doesn't tip taxi drivers and waiters enough, or he talks about himself all evening, without once asking what I think about a subject—I find I need fantasies to have an orgasm."

"What are your fantasies?" the analyst asked.

"I imagine I'm a little girl being seduced by an older man as an older woman watches. Then he has sex with her, after he is aroused by seducing me. He masturbates me with his lips on my clitoris, but doesn't put his penis inside me."

"How old are you in the fantasy?"

"About nine."

"And who is the man?"

"Some chauffeur."

"Did you ever have a chauffeur when you were little?"

"Our family had one for years. His name was Vic. He used to drive me all over. Our cook was in love with him but he married the maid."

"What do you remember about him?" the analyst asked.

"He was very handsome. Tall and blonde. And gentle and kind. He never lost his temper, no matter where we kids asked him to drive us. My mother liked him very much too."

"You've described your father as tall and blonde," said the analyst.

"Well, yes," she replied with hesitation. "But not as tall or as blonde as Vic. Or as handsome."

"Do you have any thoughts about the fantasy?"

"It's like *The Turn of the Screw*. I, the little girl, am being 'used' by the older woman and the chauffeur so he can have sex with her."

"Was that the feeling you had about your mother? That she used you to seduce your father so he would love her?"

The woman was silent. Then she said, "I did feel like a little doll as my mother dressed me in pretty clothes and then asked my father if he didn't think I was beautiful." She added, "Often my mother would make me ask my father to do things she was afraid to ask him to do. Like going for a ride in the car on Sunday. Or to take a vacation."

The analyst said, "Your tall, blonde father was the

first chauffeur in your life, wasn't he? The first to drive you around in a baby carriage. Then later, in his car."

"So *he's* the chauffeur in my sexual fantasy!" she said with sudden insight.

"Your fantasy is bisexual," the analyst commented.

"What do you mean?"

"You give yourself to the man so the older woman may have him sexually," he continued.

"I don't understand."

"You wished also to satisfy your mother sexually. Your first love, your forever love, in a sense, is your mother. Your father was second, even though your erotic feeling for him seems more intense because it is more easily remembered. And even less taboo."

Freud pointed out that the mother is the little girl's first and strongest love, that "all future loves" are modeled after this first love. If a mother provides a tender, caring love, later the girl automatically comes to accept both her love for her father and its inevitable frustration. She realizes she cannot continue to be her mother's rival for his love, and so chooses an eligible man.

One woman told her analyst that during intercourse she imagined herself an older woman seducing a blonde young man, the "handyman" in the village where she spent her summers.

"Who does the handyman remind you of?" the analyst asked.

"My younger brother," she admitted. "He is blonde. And looks a bit like my imaginary handyman."

"Did your brother and you ever engage in sexual play?" asked the analyst.

She blushed, then said, "When I was about eight years old and my brother six, we slept in the same bed, which we had never done before, when my father took us on vacation. I remembered feeling very excited as my brother and I lay down to go to sleep in the same bed. I couldn't sleep. I reached out to touch his penis, to feel what it was like. He gently pushed my hand away. I felt like a criminal."

"So you were the 'handy woman,' " the analyst said. "But in your fantasy, because the truth was too embarrassing and shameful to you, you picture your brother as the 'handy man.' "

"My father, who was a doctor, was actually the handyman around our house," she said. "He loved to fix anything that was broken. He said it relaxed him, after coping with patients all day, to come home to his machine shop in the basement where he kept toolboxes full of pliers and nails and all kinds of weird instruments."

"But the weirdest instrument of all he kept hidden from you, as did your brother," said the analyst. "And naturally you wanted to find out what it felt like, and what it did."

"I have felt so guilty all these years," she said. "Like I was trying to seduce my brother. All I wanted was to 'feel' what he was like. To find out what he had that I lacked—poor, stupid girl me."

Another woman of twenty-five, who went into therapy because she feared she might never marry, though she had sex with a number of men during the year, told her analyst, "I can't have an orgasm unless I imagine the man inside me as a Nazi soldier who has conquered my country and is now demanding that I submit to him sexually or he will kill me."

The analyst, who had heard her describe her father as a tyrant, asked, "Who, in your life, represents the Nazi soldier?"

"I guess you're referring to my father," she replied.

"The man who is taboo to you sexually," said the analyst, "and whom you have always feared because of his raging temper when he gets crossed."

While little girls do not as yet know the techniques of adult sex, they may be filled with erotic longing, a yearning to be held close, kissed, caressed by their fathers. There is nothing sexier than a little girl as she learns to use her natural wiles on her father. If a father loves his little daughter in a wise, mature way, she will not be unduly aroused. She will be able to handle her erotic feelings and eventually to transfer her sexual desire from him to a man outside the family. But if fathers, or other male adults in her life, respond in excessively erotic ways to her, she may live at too high a level of sexual tension.

One father permitted his five-year-old daughter to touch his naked penis merely because she asked if she could. A horrified friend said, "How could you seduce her in this way?" The father replied, "I'm not seducing her. I'm just satisfying her curiosity. She might as well learn about the male body from me as from some stranger." He did not understand that his behavior was very harmful to his daughter's developing sexuality, that her fantasies would be greatly stimulated at an age when emotionally she could not handle either the fantasies or her aroused physical reaction.

If a little girl is actually seduced by a man she will, as a woman, have very intense sexual fantasies because of her too early sexual arousal. One danger of early seduction, as psychoanalytic case histories show, is that the pattern of nymphomania may ensue. Girls whose fathers have been excessively seductive, just short of actual seduction, are apt to engage in much sexual acting out in later life.

Little girls may also be sexually overstimulated by mothers or other women. Freud mentioned the case of a little girl who had been masturbated almost daily by a governess, as a result of which the little girl suffered many hysterical and physical symptoms. Fantasies of women reveal there may have been a certain amount of seduction between them and their mothers.

The mother is bound to arouse some erotic desire in a little girl, not only during breast feeding in the child's first months of life, but later when she bathes and cleans the child. Mothers cannot help but rub as they wash the external genitals, which to the little girl is pleasurable. Sometimes the little girl learns to get the same pleasurable sensation by rubbing herself in bed, or learns to rub her clitoris against an object, such as a washcloth. When the Oedipal fantasies are strong, around the age of four, her incestuous dreams become connected to whatever sexual activity she is able to manage in the face of parental prohibitions.

One woman of thirty-three told her analyst that while she had sex with her husband, she would imagine her best female friend performing cunnilingus on her.

"Why do you substitute a woman for your husband in fantasy?" asked the analyst.

"It seems more exciting when a woman does it," she answered.

"Does your friend remind you of someone?"

"Come to think of it, she has the same expressive brown eyes as my mother. And she's always interested in what I do and think. Just like my mother, when I was younger."

This woman and her mother had been very close. She was an only child and her mother adored her. When she was nine, her father left home to marry his secretary, which meant that the patient and her mother were thrown even closer together, two against the harsh world. It was safer for the patient, in fantasy, to feel sexually aroused by her comforting mother than by a man, whom experience had taught her was the cruel, abandoning parent.

Another woman had the reverse fantasy: during intercourse she imagined that she was masturbating an older woman, playing both male and female roles. "During sex with a man, I fantasize I am masturbating an old lady who hasn't had sex for twenty years and is very grateful to me for giving her an orgasm," she told her analyst. Then she said she felt sorry for her mother because she had no sexual relations with a man for twenty years after she divorced her father. This patient, in fantasy, was satisfying her mother sexually, as a man would. Unconsciously she wished to take her father's place, to please her mother, so she would get her undivided love.

Wives who have intercourse with husbands who have just come from the bed of another woman, finding this exciting, are in a sense sharing the other woman in lesbian fashion. This mirrors an infantile fantasy of getting to the mother through a sharing with the father.

Another prevalent sexual fantasy of women, involving both the mother and father of childhood, is that of being a call girl or prostitute. Some women may imagine if they are "bad" they can enjoy sex, feel free to do anything they wish with a man, or allow him to do anything he wishes to them.

One wife had the fantasy she was a whore and her husband a "john" she picked up who told her he loved her because she allowed him to have oral sex with her, which his frigid wife would not permit. In her fantasy, she was the "bad" little girl who would do anything her father wanted, taking him away from her cold, unresponsive mother.

The sexual drive in women undergoes a complicated development as "vicissitudes," to use Freud's word, occur, causing frustration and anger in a growing girl. She must eventually accept that her desire for her father is destined to remain forever unfulfilled. Sometimes a father does not make this easy for her. A mother may punish a daughter "for what are the consequences of the other parent's unrecognized temptation," in the words of Dr. Sandor Rado. Some fathers arouse their daughters' sexual desires; the mother then becomes jealous and takes it out on the daughter.

A daughter's natural erotic desire for her father comes into conflict with her dependency on her mother and father. She is, in a sense, caught between the Scylla of her passion and the Charybdis of her need to hide her feelings so her mother and father will continue to love and take care of her. This helps her in the resolution of the Oedipal conflict.

The rape fantasy is a quite common sexual fantasy of women, with the father of childhood portrayed as the brutal attacker, though usually in the disguise of another man. Why, in the conscious fantasies of so many women, is the lover a sadist who tortures, beats, or rapes them? This beating fantasy has its origin in the woman's incestuous attachment to her father, Freud reported in his historic paper, "A Child Is Being Beaten."

In their psychic reality many women prefer the brutal man who will overpower them sexually to the reasonable, tender, thoughtful bedmate. The brutal man is thrilling sexually since he represents the father of childhood who, in a woman's unconscious, appeared cruel because he would not seduce his daughter and give up his wife at a time his daughter desired him with her whole heart. The cruel stranger also takes total responsibility for the sexual act; a woman has only to give in to him, submit to his will, thereby erasing all guilt over her incestuous wishes.

The original fantasy in "A Child Is Being Beaten," Freud says, is, "I am being beaten (i.e., I am loved) by my father." This is later replaced by a fantasy which disavows the little girl's wish for sexual intimacy with her father.

The beating is then performed in her imagination upon someone she views with jealous rage as she becomes a spectator of an event that takes the place of a sexual act. She imagines the sexual act as a beating for, to her, it resembles one from her early impressions of her mother and father in bed.

Fantasies of rape also arise due to the childhood notion that sex is a sadistic attack on a woman's body. This may result from the child's having seen or heard the parents in sexual intercourse. It is not unusual for a little girl to be aware of sights and sounds emanating from her parents' bedroom, and to construct fantasies to explain acts she does not understand, fantasies on the level of her sensory feelings, depending whether she is in the oral, anal, or phallic stage.

One young woman told her analyst, "Before I go to bed every night I lock all the windows. Then I look under the bed and in every closet to make sure no one has stolen in during the day. I always leave a light in the living room to scare off burglars. I have two strong locks on my door but I still go to bed afraid someone will break the window and steal in at night and try to rape and rob me, maybe kill me. I can't help it. The feeling is so strong I can't control it."

Her fear masks the wish to be raped (burglarized) and also clearly reveals the fantasy that sex is sadistic, that she must suffer at the hands of a brutal man.

Nora Ephron describes a recurring sexual fantasy in her book *Crazy Salad:* the fantasy's "broad outline," she explains, "has largely to do with being dominated by faceless males who rip my clothes off. That's just about all they have to do. Stare at me in this faceless way, go mad with desire, and rip my clothes off. It's terrific. In my sex fantasy, nobody ever loves me for my mind."

Lynn Roth, director of comedy development for Twentieth-Century-Fox and author of the monodrama

Freud, says, "The fantasy of rape is erotic if there's a man in a three-piece suit with whom I'm intimately involved. Someone who appears very sophisticated and controlled on the surface but who unleashes great passion within the confines of the bedroom."

Ultimately, no woman, no matter how brilliant, wants to be desired for anything but her beautiful face and body; all the compliments in the world about her intellectual achievements, while they bolster her ego, do not gratify her passionate, primitive impulses.

A woman's incestuous love for her father "cannot avoid the fate of repression," wrote Freud, as disillusionment sets in—perhaps because of unexpected slights by her father, or by the birth of a brother or sister which she experiences as an act of faithlessness and betrayal. Or perhaps because the little girl's yearning for her father remains unsatisfied too long. At the time of repression, a sense of guilt appears in connection with the incestuous wishes and fantasies now buried in the unconscious.

Beating fantasies represent not only punishment for forbidden incestuous relations, but also the regressive substitute for it. "Here for the first time we have the essence of masochism," Freud says.

He explains that masochism is the transformation of an active sadistic impulse into the passive wish to suffer, due to a sense of guilt. The guilt in women that follows masturbation is connected not with the act itself, but with the fantasy that lies at its root—the incestuous wish for the father.

On the basis of Freud's theory of masochism, it can be understood how, out of a sense of guilt over her sexual feelings toward her father, repressed since childhood, a woman will choose a sexual partner who is cruel to her, who beats her either physically or psychically. In the deepest sense, she is living out her early erotic fantasies.

This explains the later adult perversions in which actual beatings are needed by a woman to reach a genital climax. Because of the intensity of her early incestuous wishes and the consequent need to be punished for them, she cannot reach orgasm until a man who is the substitute for her father provides the proper punishment.

The above is true for men as well. "It has an ugly sound and is paradoxical as well, but nevertheless it must be said that whoever is to be really free and happy in love must have overcome his deference for women and come to terms with the idea of incest with mother or sister." Freud was speaking about men, but his remarks also apply to women: a woman must overcome her "deference" for men and come to terms with the idea of incest with father or brother, for "deference" conceals hatred.

"Anyone who in the face of this test subjects himself to serious self-examination will indubitably find that at the bottom of his heart he regards the sexual act as something degrading, which soils and contaminates not only the body," said Freud. "And he will only be able to look for the origin of this attitude, which he will certainly not willingly acknowledge, in that period of his youth in which his sexual passions were already strongly developed but in which gratification of them with an object outside the family was almost as completely prohibited as with an incestuous one."

Freud explained that what he called "moral masochism" was the sexualization of the sadistic impulse. The woman seeks to suffer as punishment for her original wish to take her father from her mother, which carries with it the wish her mother were dead.

A number of women imagine they are being spanked, rather than beaten, in order to become sexually aroused. Freud said one of the fantasies connected with spankings and beatings is that the father is masturbating the child—which the little girl desires him to do.

One woman told her therapist, "Nothing arouses me more than imagining that after he has undressed and I have undressed, a man walks towards me as I lie on the bed, gently turns me over and spanks me before he puts his penis inside me. I am always ready for him after the spanking."

"Did your father spank you as a little girl?" her analyst asked.

"He sure did," she said. "He often reminded me that when I was two years old, he spanked me to stop me from wetting the bed at night. And when I was about eight, I remember he spanked me when I stole some money out of my mother's pocketbook to buy candy. And again when I dared fight with him about where I wanted to go to camp."

"Spankings arouse children sexually," the analyst said. "As well as instilling in them a feeling of anger and desire for revenge."

Even with today's new sexual freedom, women usually do not use obscene words during the sexual act, as men sometimes do. Most women object to so-called dirty words in bed, feeling these words are deprecating. Indeed, psychoanalysts agree that tender, loving words are more appropriate during lovemaking. Obscene words indicate a man thinks of the woman as a whore. He does this so he can deny his sexual fantasies center on his mother, the "good" woman. Such a man, according to Freud, splits off all his tabooed sensuous urges toward his mother and during sexual intimacies "avoids all association with feelings of tenderness."

The ability to express tenderness is very important in achieving mature, or genital love, Freud believed. If a man or woman has an irreconcilable split between sensual and tender feelings, this will cause their erotic life to remain, as he put it, "divided between two channels: the same two that are personified in art as heavenly and earthly (or animal) love."

He described it further: "Where such men love they have no desire and where they desire they cannot love. In order to keep their sensuality out of contact with the objects they love, they seek out objects whom they need not love; and, in accordance with the laws of the 'sensitivity of complexes' and the 'return of the repressed,' the strange refusal implied in psychical impotence is made whenever the objects selected in order to avoid incest possess some trait, often quite inconspicuous, reminiscent of the objects that must be avoided."

Just as there are men who can express love only "for a harlot," to use Freud's phrase, so there are women who can love only promiscuous men—Don Juans. But not until these women have some occasion for jealousy does their passion reach its height and the man acquire his full value. Such women are, in fantasy, reliving the childhood Oedipal triangle. They are for the moment successful in mastering the conflict as they keep their promiscuous lover (the father) by their side and triumph over their rival (the mother). That their lover will inevitably discard them, as he has all his other women, is unconsciously known even as they consciously fight against all odds to keep him sexually faithful.

The woman who loves a Don Juan also believes her lover needs her to "rescue" him from his unhappy life, that she must save him from a fate worse than death— promiscuity. She wishes to protect him from his own evil impulses. Here she is displaying pre-Oedipal feelings, the inverted wish that her own mother would have "protected" her from her passionate desire for her father.

Some of the new sexual practices believed by many to exemplify greater freedom actually prove the existence of the old incestuous fantasies at work in a different way.

Orgies, for instance, in which couples perform the sexual act with different partners and in full view of each other, are simply a re-enactment of the primal scene, the child getting even with parents for having intercourse in front of him (or in the room next to him, where he could over-hear sounds and words). When three persons are involved, this too relates to the primal scene, with the child in the adult at last able to fulfill his wish to join his mother and father in the act of sex.

Occasionally girls take part in what is known as a "gang bang," an uninterrupted series of sexual encounters by one female with a group of males. Though such behavior is usually associated with violence and rape, some girls enjoy this form of sexual encounter, and even invite it. Dr. Walter Stewart explains some of the girls' motivation:

"Part of it is the illicit quality—doing something that is considered bad, forbidden. This ties into the idea of masturbation. Then, too, in the unconscious, the many men represent one person, the girl's father, so that taking on all the men in fantasy is a way of taking on the father. Also, there is the wish to lose control in the sense of not having the act terminated, but an endless procession of penises, of which, therefore, none are destroyed and none become flaccid. The act has the quality of being surrounded by many penises, tying in with the Medusa head of snakes. The girl takes on the boys unconsciously as a way of destroying them, so the act is also aggressive; the violence, as assumed, does not always come from the boys."

There are women who, out of their hatred of men and their fear of being penetrated, avoid men and prefer to get sexual release from masturbating. These women, whom Marie Bonaparte calls "clitoridals," suffer, no matter how much they may deny it, she claims. They never are able to surrender to "a mutual passion." Though such women maintain they are independent and self-sufficient, when it comes to sexuality, they pay a high price for their isolated sexual activity.

A recent nationwide study of female sexuality, *The Hite Report* (by Shere Hite, written in cooperation with the New York Chapter of the National Organization for Women), describes a four-year study during which a questionnaire about their sexual problems was sent to 3,000 women between the ages of fourteen and seventy-eight. Seventy percent of the women reported they did not experience orgasm during intercourse. The report also revealed that direct clitoral stimulation is necessary for a majority of women to achieve orgasm even during intercourse.

The current feminist philosophy that masturbation allows a woman to understand her body and to have a sense of control over her own sexual expression is opposed by most psychoanalysts, who believe that women who resort to masturbation do so out of childhood fantasies that block the enjoyment of mature sexual intimacy.

Masturbation during adolescence is natural, serving not only to release sexual tension but "the much more subtle function of enabling the young woman undergoing rapid physiological changes to become truly acquainted with her body and the sensations it is capable of producing," according to Rhoda Lorand, who treats and writes about adolescents.

"Moderate amounts of masturbation are considered to be of importance to the development of the sense of self in adolescence," she says. "Total absence of masturbation during adolescence indicates an overwhelming fear of dealing with sexual drives. This can be produced by severe prohibitions against childish auto-eroticism, or exaggerated fear of damaging the genitals."

Ms. Lorand tells of a very intelligent woman who, all through her school life, had suffered from a learning disability, believing it resulted from brain damage caused by masturbation during adolescence. "Almost the whole of her life had been spent under the shadow of this mistaken belief, which was now beginning to spread to her handling of her children. She was terrified lest anyone tickle the youngsters, believing the sexual desire thus aroused would lead them to uncontrollable masturbation and they would then share her fate."

This woman had lost her mother at the age of five and, thereafter, as Lorand puts it, "repeatedly sought solace in her own body for the disappointments she experienced in her longings for love and affection, ignored by an indifferent and harassed stepmother." Her whole personality was stamped by the effects of her unsuccessful struggle with masturbation, and she suffered intense feelings of inferiority and worthlessness because of her guilt.

Can masturbation be regarded as an adequate method of gratification for the adult sexual drive? Lorand's answer: "Masturbation is considered normal in infancy and childhood when it would not be normal to have a sex relationship with another person, less so in puberty when it is possible to gratify sexual desire with another person, and no longer normal in adulthood except under circumstances of abnormal deprivation."

She adds, "Our society encourages masturbation beyond the years when it would be considered a satisfactory method of gratifying the sexual drive, because we do not officially allow our adolescents to become adults sexually, although we do encourage adult behavior in all other respects."

Too frequent masturbation, or compulsive masturbation in an adolescent "indicates overly strong ties to infantile behavior," Lorand says. Prolonged masturbation may make the finding of a suitable sexual partner more diffi-

cult. "Since masturbation requires no effort, it can delay
the felt need to find a mate; thus, normal adjustment to
reality is retarded," she asserts. "Furthermore, since no
real person can measure up to the idealized creatures of
fantasy, the giving up of fantasy figures for the acceptance
of real people can be seriously delayed, encouraging a
generalized retreat from reality and too great a reliance
upon make-believe."

Sometimes excessive masturbation in a young woman
represents an escape from lesbian leanings, she points out,
as the young woman fears being tempted into a homosex-
ual affair and tries to safeguard against it by masturbation.

It is not uncommon for girls just entering adolescence
to be entirely preoccupied with the sensations their ma-
nipulation of the sex organs is able to yield, Lorand maintains. But if girls well into adolescence engage in
masturbation without requiring the presence in their
thoughts of a young man, they are not experiencing
"quasi-action in fantasy," a step toward heterosexual activity, Lorand says, and it can therefore be assumed that
important psychological aspects of their sexual development have been blocked.

She mentions the aftermath of feelings of "malaise"
in masturbation. One theory maintains that the malaise is
a psychosomatic response to feelings of guilt, anxiety, and
shame which accompany masturbation to some degree in
everyone. Another theory argues that masturbation is, at
best, "an incomplete experience for anyone who has
become capable of a mature sexual experience with a
partner, and therefore leaves a residue of undischarged
tension and frustration which contines to have a disturbing effect upon the person in the form of a psychosomatic
response (illness brought on by emotional disturbance)."

Freud himself called masturbation "the executive
agent of infantile sexuality." It is indulged in by those
who, because of inner conflicts, have been unable to move

out of childhood sexual expression into the mutuality of adult sexual love. *The Hite Report* reveals that most women who masturbate, while getting physical satisfaction in the loner's way, feel very guilty. Masturbation always creates guilt, since the basic fantasy accompanying it contains the wish from the woman's childhood to be erotically loved by her father. The seductive or sadistic man of the fantasy is her father in disguised form.

A woman may, all her life, prefer masturbation, which she can control, to accepting the sexual satisfaction provided by a man, which is beyond her control and may mean sexual frustration. Such a woman has not moved out of the dependency of childhood, fearing sexual penetration by a man. She is still living in an inner world inhabited only by her mother and herself. Before a woman can accept her natural Oedipal feelings for her father, she must be able to separate in a psychic sense from her mother, not remain a clinging child.

One woman, who never married, lived alone and depended on masturbation for sexual release. Her mother had lost a baby in childbirth and transmitted to her a feeling of terror about giving birth. She had the fantasy she would die if she ever became pregnant. This fantasy mitigated against her being able to trust a man sexually— in her mind she feared the man as an enemy who would make her pregnant and cause her death. She watched television every night after she came home from her job as executive in a large department store. She would sit quietly for hours in a large chair in front of the television set as a phantom voice talked to her, soothed her, entertained her, made love for her, murdered for her. Even though she held a responsible job, unconsciously she remained a passive child, living in an unreal world inhabited by herself and the voices coming to her from the television set, which represented the all-giving mother of her childhood.

Women who are married to sexually inept men often masturbate to get sexual release, with their fantasies supplying the way. Certainly their lives would be more satisfactory if they had chosen partners who could satisfy them sexually. But because of conflict stemming from childhood, these women are unable to make a wise sexual choice of mates. Fantasies do serve an important purpose, permitting sexual outlet where otherwise there might be none. Women ought not to feel ashamed of their fantasies, no matter what they may be.

It is better to be able to release sexual tension through whatever means are possible than to live in frustration and repression. Nevertheless, it is far better still to be able to achieve orgasm without fantasy, to face one's sexual partner as a human being, not as a figment of one's imagination. A woman cheats herself of intimacy with a man when she has to fantasize he is someone else. She also cheats herself of the full emotional enjoyment possible in the sexual act. If she needs to fantasize during intercourse, she is "converting a two-person situation into an emotional solo performance," according to psychoanalyst Dr. Marc Hollender.

Another psychoanalyst adds: "Fantasy blocks out the man as a partner, substituting the father of childhood. The woman not only blocks out the man but her full emotional and sexual feelings. She limits her emotional response to that of a little girl who wants her father in bed with her."

A woman will lose herself in the act of sex, no need for fantasy, if she is emotionally healthy, agrees Dr. Henriette Klein. A woman's need for fantasy stems in part from her inhibitions, caused by the sexual restrictions of society and her parents, and in part by the fear of her Oedipal feelings, Dr. Klein explains.

The use of accompanying fantasies places sex on a masturbatory level, for only the self is involved in a secret, titillating sense. One woman, after therapy, became aware of the difference between lovemaking with the aid of fantasy and without. The latter gave her the conscious feeling her partner was himself—a man she loved.

As a result of therapy, of facing both the conscious and underlying unconscious sexual fantasies that had formerly brought her to orgasm, she was able to have sex without fantasy. She found her physical and emotional reactions far more intense and fulfilling. "It's a new freedom," she told her analyst. "Freedom to really share sex with a man, not use him as a way of masturbating."

If a little girl is ashamed of her feelings of love for her father, she is apt, as a woman, to be ashamed of those feelings for another man. She must learn to accept as natural her love for her father, a love that is sensual as well as emotional and intellectual. It is a love to which she is entitled. But she must also go one step further. She must be able to accept the frustration of this love, of her wish to take her father from her mother. This she will do if her mother and father help her accept both her feelings of love and the anger aroused by its frustration. She must not be allowed to live with the illusion that she is "Daddy's favorite." Reality is harsh and the sooner she can accept this, the happier she will be in later life.

Dreams of desire unlimited float unabashedly in the unconscious of all little girls, buried along the way to womanhood, but never really stilled. To understand their origin and the feelings they inspired is to take away their danger. Uncovering her earliest, most primitive love objects gives a woman the chance to bestow her adult love on the man most likely to give her sexual and other satisfactions.

Chapter 4

"ANYTHING HE CAN DO, I CAN DO BETTER"

One of the fantasies preventing a woman from being sexually happy with a man revolves around the wish to *be* a man. With the growing acceptance of equal rights, a woman's wish for power and success, believed for centuries to be manly achievements, may lead to unhappiness if that wish arises out of the competitive fantasies of childhood. For there is a very important difference between a woman who is unconsciously *driven* to power and success and one who consciously *chooses* those goals.

One young woman, a newspaper reporter, confessed that her fantasy is "to write the great American novel and have hundreds of thousands of dollars so I can travel all over the world. That, to me, is success. I would then envy no one." Such success has in fact been achieved by a number of women, among them Ruth West, who for many years worked diligently for a moderate income. One day a publisher who knew she had written two diet books asked her to find a physician willing to work with her on a new kind of diet. After a long and careful search, she found Dr. Robert C. Atkins, and collaborated with him on *Dr. Atkins' Diet Revolution.* The book's phenomenal sales made Ms. West financially independent. Unlike the newspaper reporter, however, she arrived at success through a good deal of hard work over the years, which finally paid off in the execution of an original idea. Ruth West *chose* the way to success and was not desperately driven to it.

A woman's wish to succeed, to become powerful, aside from showing a healthy aggressive drive, may also contain the desire to destroy men. Many women, as they compete professionally with men, show a castrating quality in their behavior that makes it impossible for them to enjoy the success they do achieve. They feel basically frustrated, sensing they are not getting what they really want.

Women who have never come to terms with their unconscious wish to be a man usually do not choose lovers or husbands who will be protectors but passive men who, as a rule, have the unconscious wish to be a woman. Each seeks in the other the fulfillment of a fantasy deriving from infancy. Such relationships rarely work, for whenever an adult makes infantile demands, it is impossible for another adult to fulfill them.

With a sense of power supposedly comes an increase in self-esteem. It is as if power, success, and wealth automatically evoke the feeling, "I am good, I am loved, and I did it all myself—I don't need anyone, man or woman. I am complete in myself." We view power as protection against dependency on others: if a woman is powerful enough, famous enough, successful enough, rich enough,

she is beyond any hurt mortal man can inflict; she is suffi-
cient unto herself.

But for a woman to want inordinate power, success,
and wealth at the expense of ignoring her emotional and
sexual needs indicates, according to psychoanalysts, that
she unconsciously wishes to be a man. She is still dominated by the girl-child fantasy that, if only she had been
born a boy, life would be far more pleasurable. Such a
wish is not surprising, in view of women's low status in
society throughout the ages. That status cannot but enhance the popular fantasy that if she had been born a boy,
all opportunities open to men would be available to her,
including sexual freedom.

This fantasy from childhood contains at its core the
wish for a penis and the belief that the only way for the
girl to get one is to take it away from a man (originally her
father—the only man she knew in her circumscribed life
as a child).

We have only to watch and listen to the talk of little
girls to become aware of this wish. One four-year-old said
to her father as she saw him diaper her newborn brother,
"Why is he so fancy and I'm so plain?" A six-year-old girl
told a social worker at a settlement house, "I'm growing
a penis under my arm so I can be like my brother. No one
will see it but I'll know it's there." And Dr. Karl Abraham,
pioneer psychoanalyst, told of a two-year-old girl who
opened a box of cigars, took one out, and brought it to her
father, after which she went back to the box, picked up
another cigar, and handed it to her mother. Returning to
the box, she took out a third cigar and held it so that it
protruded from the lower part of her body. She was expressing, Abraham said, her wish that her father give her
a penis. By also handing her mother a cigar she was saying
that she, "as a little woman," might hope to get a penis.

The wish to grow a penis is apparent in the dreams

of many women. One wife dreamed she had grown a
penis and was proudly showing it to her husband. Another
woman dreamed she walked into a store where penises
were on display, and prepared to pick one out for herself.

The fantasy of being a "changeling," of undergoing a
metamorphosis that will bring happiness, reveals the wish
in women to be different, to be transformed into men.
This was vividly illustrated by the comment of one young
woman on an NBC television program entitled *Women
Risking Change,* aired on November 20, 1976. She said
she was eager to change her mode of life and, as she put
it, to "dust off the cobwebs, open the closet door, and pull
it out." What does one "pull out" but a penis? Another
woman on the program said, voicing the wish of many a
woman, "I just don't want to be the kind of woman my
mother was." On the most primitive level she wanted to
change her genitals to those of a man.

It is the fantasy of many a woman that she can trans-
form herself into something else, usually a more sexy,
beautiful being. As one woman of thirty-three said, "My
looks are just average. I have wanted to be different all my
life. I envy the tall, slim, glamorous woman. Every time
I look in the mirror and see my unglamorous face and
figure, I could cry."

This is the adult version of the little girl's wish to turn
from ugly duckling into graceful swan. According to Web-
ster's *New World Dictionary,* a changeling is "a child
secretly put in the place of another; any ugly, queer, idiotic or bad-tempered child, superstitiously explained
away as being a substitute child left by the fairies for a
child stolen by them."

The little girl may have this fantasy in reverse. She
believes she was stolen from her rightful parents and
forced to live with "ugly, queer, idiotic or bad-tempered"
parents, and that her real mother and father were of no-

ble origin, wealthy, and, in addition, warm and loving. This, in Freud's words, is "the family romance." Its origin as fantasy lies in the little girl's very strong wish to deny her incestuous feelings for her mother and father, as well as to deny what she thinks is their cruelty to her, and her subsequent anger. If she is a changeling, or if they are not her real parents, she need not feel guilty about either her sexual or aggressive wishes toward her mother and father.

One little girl stormed at her mother, "I don't have to obey. You're not my *real* mother."

The mother was at first shocked, then amused. She asked, "Who do you think is your real mother?"

"Mrs. Tucker," said the little girl, naming the mother of her best friend. "She's always nice to me."

"But Mrs. Tucker is Molly's mother," said the little girl's mother.

"Mine, too," the little girl insisted. "*She* never yells at me. Or gives me orders."

The idea of becoming part of someone else's family, of turning into a different kind of child, or gaining another sort of parent, is carried over into adulthood in those women who unconsciously seek in a man the accepting, kind, thoughtful parent they never had as a little girl. Such women expect marriage to solve all their conflicts, look on their husbands not as human beings, with all the faults of a human being, but as the "perfect" parent they lacked.

Along with the changeling fantasy goes the rescue fantasy. Both emanate from the little girl's wish that someone strong will come along to rescue her from her wretched parents. Some women live as though this fantasy were still possible to achieve, waiting for someone to magically appear and help them find the answers to life.

One divorced woman, looking for work as an interior

decorator, said, "Someone will come along and offer me a partnership or some fabulous house or apartment to design. All I have to do is wait." She asked all her friends to find her clients, depending on the kindness of others for her livelihood.

The woman who must be the rescuer, who keeps busy helping other people out of their plights, is also showing a strong wish to be rescued. She resorts to the psychological defense Freud named "reaction formation." Her act of "rescuing" masks the underlying wish to be rescued. She is saying, "I am doing unto you what I wish were done unto me."

Showing similar behavior, missionaries who set out to save the world are really saying, "I wish to be saved." This was eloquently shown in *Rain,* Somerset Maugham's story about Sadie Thompson and the Reverend Alfred Davidson. Those who identify with God, who perform God's work, who "do good," are saying they wished their parents had "done good" by them as children. They are also denying all "evil, devilish" feelings for, after all, God fights the Devil.

Reaction formation is also seen in phobias. The woman who washes her hands excessively does so because she is afraid of "dirty" thoughts, usually the wish to masturbate, which "dirties" the hands. Any symptom that is excessive tells of some buried wish or fantasy expressed by the symptom.

Abraham reported that psychoanalytic studies showed "a great number of women have repressed the wish to be male; we come across this wish in all products of the unconscious, especially in dreams and neurotic symptoms. The extraordinary frequency of these observations suggests that this wish is one common to and occurring in all women." Freud was the first to make this observation and to write on the subject of "penis envy."

One twenty-eight-year-old woman in analysis became aware of her wish to have a penis after reading a comic book about monsters to her three-year-old son. She noticed every time a monster appeared in a picture or she mentioned the word "monster" her son would touch his penis, partly in excitement but also in apprehension, as though to make sure it was still there. He was both sexually excited at the menacing monsters and yet feared the "monsters" in his life—his mother and father, who might take his penis away if he was "bad" (had sexual or aggressive feelings or fantasies).

That night the woman dreamed her childhood dentist had drugged her and pulled out a perfectly healthy tooth. In horror she asked why he had done so, but he only leered at her. When she woke, she realized the connection between the dream and the events of the previous night. She remembered the "monster" book she had read to her son, then his gesture of protecting his penis. She realized this had stirred thoughts in her own mind of the childhood wish to have a penis, and the illusion that a dentist, who, when she was little removed an infected tooth, had "pulled out" or "cut out" her fantasied penis. The dentist represented her father and mother, who hid pennies under her pillow when her baby teeth fell out, as though to restore the tooth (the penis, in the little girl's unconscious). Her underlying fantasy was that her parents had "pulled out" or "cut off" the penis she once had. The contemporary dream expressed fulfillment of her infantile wish to get back the penis she believed taken from her.

Describing what he calls "the castration complex" in women, Abraham maintains that a large number of them fail to successfully repress and sublimate the childhood wish to be a boy. They continue to believe the fantasy that the female genital is a "wound." They feel damaged, mutilated, "robbed," as though something has been stolen from them. They wish to revenge themselves on the man, who is regarded as privileged. Their impulse is to castrate the man, to take his penis for themselves, thereby rendering themselves whole.

As little girls grow older, they naturally bury their wish for a penis deep in their memory. But the persistence of the unconscious wish is proved in those girls who become tomboys, who compete scholastically with boys, and later compete professionally and sexually with men.

One woman of thirty said her girlhood wish to be a boy was hardly unconscious: "I really *wanted*, with my whole heart, to be a boy." She imitated a boy's walk, threw a baseball as hard and accurately as a boy, and became an outstanding athlete in high school. "But," she added, "at the same time I was very feminine. I loved party dresses. I spent hours having my hair curled at the beauty parlor. And I had lots of beaux."

She exemplifies the girl whose basic desire is to be feminine, but who also envies and emulates boys. This wish automatically carries with it the wish to have a body like a boy. According to Freud, every little girl has the fantasy that she once had a penis, just like a boy, but that it was taken from her by her mother for being "bad" or in some way misbehaving. When menstruation begins, the bleeding confirms the girl's fantasy that the penis she was born with was "cut off." She feels hurt, angry, deprived. She believes she has an "imperfect" body, a piece missing. She may spend the rest of her life trying to be "perfect," to achieve the coveted penis—an impossible dream.

One young woman said to her analyst, "I have always wanted to be the 'perfect' lady. I see now that, unconsciously, 'perfect' to me meant 'with a penis.' A perfect lady meant a phallic lady."

St. Thomas Aquinas called woman "a misbegotten male." Centuries later, after observing and listening to male patients, and delving into his own unconscious, Freud said he believed man's treatment of women as inferior masked man's own inner terror each time he looked at the body of a woman and realized it lacked a penis. This aroused his deepest fear—castration. His contempt of the female body arose in defense against that fear.

Women themselves have long accepted this masculine bias. They have even outdone men in self-depreciation, thereby colluding in their age-old subjugation. As a result of such feelings of inferiority, woman envies and fears man's sexual and physical power, submits to him out of that fear, and then feels an underlying contempt for him, just as he does for her. Her only measure of revenge is this contempt—the slave is permitted to feel contempt for her brutal master as long as she does not reveal it and incur her master's hate.

In matriarchal societies women have tried to dominate as they imitate the overthrown, psychologically castrated males, assuming their power. Rather than believing men to be partners, the Amazons openly sought to defeat and subjugate them, unlike most women who, over the centuries, have had to hide all desire for revenge.

Freud did not maintain, as he has so often been accused, that all women envy and try to destroy men or that their whole lives constitute a vain search for a phantom penis. He did state that women often experience conflicts because of the struggle between normal feminine impulses and the wish to be "a man"—to be superior, live more freely, and enjoy greater sexual pleasure.

Freud fully granted the deleterious influence of society in this struggle of women. He wrote that the long abstinence from sexuality "forced" on Victorian women and "the lingering of their sensuality in phantasy" make it exceedingly difficult "for them later on to undo the connection thus formed in their minds between sensual activities and something forbidden, and they turn out to be psychically impotent, *i.e.,* frigid, when at last such activities do become permissible." He further stated that "the long period of delay between sexual maturity and sexual activity which is demanded by education for social reasons" creates in both women and men a kind of "psychical impotence resulting from the lack of union between tenderness and sensuality."

Freud divided women into three types, each responding differently to the traumatic shock which, he said, every little girl experiences on first realizing the difference between the sexes.

The first type of woman soon succeeds in transforming the desire for a penis into that of a child by her father, and eventually another man. She becomes a "normal, maternal woman" with the ability to have vaginal orgasms. The second type suspends all sexual activity and abandons competition with men, "feeling themselves too unequal socially and psychically, achieving a status in society similar to the workers in the anthill or hive." The third type shows "a defiant overemphasis of masculinity" and clings to "the psychical and organic male elements innate in all women: the masculinity complex and the clitoris." Usually, Freud added, the three types are rarely found alone in a single woman but combined. It is the predominance of elements of one type over the other that influences her personality, he stated.

According to Joan Riviere (a student of Freud and later a lay analyst in London), one defense of women who wish they were men is "to put on a mask of womanliness to avert anxiety and the retribution feared from men." This "womanliness" serves "both to hide the possession of masculinity and to avert the reprisals expected if a woman was found to possess it—much as a thief will turn out his pockets and ask to be searched to prove that he has not the stolen goods."

Such women lead "apparently happy lives" with husbands, achieving sexual orgasm, though the gratification it brings is "of the nature of a reassuring and restitution of something lost [the phantom penis], and not ultimately pure enjoyment." Riviere concludes, "The man's love gives her back her self-esteem."

The desire to be masculine may also stem from another source, Riviere points out, in that "as always, with girls, the mother is the more hated, and consequently the more feared. She will execute the punishment that fits the crime—destroy the girl's body, her beauty, her children, her capacity for having children, mutilate her, devour her, torture her and kill her. In this appalling predicament the girl's only safety lies in placating the mother and atoning for her crime. She must retire from rivalry with the mother and if she can, endeavor to restore to her what she has stolen."

The girl, who in such a case has identified with her father, then uses her desire to be a man "by *putting it at the service of the mother*," Riviere states. "She becomes the father, and takes his place; so she can 'restore' him to the mother." This constitutes one of the most common fantasies of little girls: if they had a penis they could be men and therefore sexually satisfy their mothers, instead of competing with them, which they fear to do. They believe the mother will mutilate, torture, and kill them in revenge for their incestuous wishes. This reflects also the little girls' fantasy-wish of what they would like to do to their mothers.

Freud noted "in the course of some women's lives there is a repeated alternation between periods in which masculinity or femininity gains the upper hand." Further: "Some portion of what we men call 'the enigma of women' may perhaps be derived from this expression of bisexuality in women's lives."

He also pointed out that the sexual development of a woman is complicated by the presence of two main zones of erotic pleasure, the clitoris and the vagina. Until the phallic phase, the clitoris is the center of a girl's masturbatory activity. She renounces clitoral masturbation when, under the influence of penis envy and a change to feminine orientation, she repudiates her mother and turns to her father with the Oedipal wish for a child, replacing her earlier wish for a penis.

Freud believed "the sexual function of many women is crippled by their obstinately clinging to this clitoris excitability so that they remain anesthetic in coitus." Dr. Helene Deutsch said of the woman who has difficulty in experiencing vaginal orgasms: "What is in question here is not at all the so frequently overstressed and even ridiculous demands made upon men . . . that they heighten the woman's erotic excitability (in the physical sense) by their dexterity. *The road to the feminine woman as a sexual object leads through the psyche.*" (Italics mine.) This is why all the sex manuals in the world cannot give a woman emotional fulfillment in sex even if she gets release from physical tension.

Some women, though they succeed in changing their love object from their mother to their father, will sexually desire women. They still "cling tenaciously to the dominantly phallic erotic zone and, with that organ, essentially male and inappropriate to the feminine function, will love and desire love objects that are female," says Marie Bonaparte, who maintains that bisexuality is at the root of penis envy and the original libidinal impulses.

Bonaparte claims "we are justified in thinking that

libidinal fixation on the clitoris, in woman, when tenaciously maintained, corresponds to a basically biological masculine character incorporated in the feminine organism." When women masturbate, usually a fantasy masculine figure is involved, with whom they identify. They play the part of the man, as well as the woman, as they give themselves sexual satisfaction, using finger or some article or instrument as substitute for the man's penis.

To be able to love a woman in later life, a boy must be able to love a creature who is whole yet without a phallus—a woman—and he must never accept the loss of his own penis. Whereas a girl, to become a woman, "must normally accept the loss of that penis," Bonaparte concludes. "The woman, who, *per contra,* through jealousy of the male penis and revenge against its male possessor, psychically seeks to tear it from him, deprive him of it and thus, by a sort of talion [the law of the talion—an eye for an eye] project her own castration on the male, is thereby preparing herself to reject a loving acceptation of the male penis, whence will arise divers forms of hysterical frigidity through the repression of acceptant vaginal response," she claims.

To achieve ultimate femininity women must have changed both their dominant infantile clitoridal erotic zone and their original love object, the mother, Freud maintained. "The carrying over of emotional attachment from the mother as an object to the father, constitutes, indeed, the essential feature in the development of femininity," he said.

Noting that the Oedipal phase is preceded by a phase "in which there is an exclusive attachment to the mother of like intensity and ardor," Freud comments: "Since many women give us the impression that their mature life is engrossed in a struggle with their husband just as their youth was spent in contention with their mother, we may conclude ... that the girl's hostile attitude toward her mother is not a result of rivalry in the Oedipus complex, but that it arises in an earlier phase and is merely reinforced and used in the Oedipus situation."

The reason many women prefer the clitoral orgasm to the vaginal is their underlying fear of penetration, according to Dr. Walter A. Stewart, author of *Psychoanalysis: The First Ten Years.* The fantasy that penetration by a man means mutilation or death arises in childhood. The female perversions have as their basis the fear of the penis as an instrument that will maim or kill them as it penetrates.

Penis envy is not a life-long state to which women are doomed, he points out, but "a regressive fixation in women afraid of their femininity." The wish to be a man remains a driving one only if a woman is afraid of sexual penetration by a man or of pregnancy.

Women who have a horror of being sexually penetrated may in their sexual fantasies symbolically represent the penis as something they can control and that will not harm them—the fingers and tongues of their sexual partners, for example, or a similarly shaped object. Dr. Melanie Klein holds that "the true major feminine anxiety is a fear of internal bodily injury."

Women also fear the "letting go" in sex which, in fantasy, may imply they will not be able to control their aggression toward the man, says Dr. Stewart. They fear they may even bite off his penis as they once wished to bite off their mother's breast when they became angry at her.

A little girl's yearning for a penis may be very intense in a family where both mother and father favor a brother or in some way convey the feeling they wish the girl had been a boy. This is especially true if the first-born is a girl or if there have been several girls and the expected newborn turns out to be another girl instead of the wished-for boy. The girl wants to be loved *as a little girl.* Otherwise she will never feel feminine or worthy of being loved. If she does not think she is loved for herself, the only way of winning her parents' affection is to try to behave like a boy.

Many a woman believes that if she were a man she would experience greater sexual pleasure, being in control of her own orgasms instead of feeling frustrated at times (perhaps always, in some instances). As a little girl, according to psychoanalysts, a woman had the fantasy that because a boy's penis is bigger than her clitoris, the boy gets greater pleasure when he masturbates. In her mind, "the bigger, the better." This fantasy carries over, unconsciously, into adulthood.

Women also have the fantasy that if they had a penis they could, like a man, urinate without "messing" themselves. Their shame often is based on memories of their mothers' negative reactions when they were being toilet-trained. They imagine too that if they had been born a boy they would not have to endure what they think of as the shame and humiliation of menstruation. Some young girls become extremely frightened when they experience their first period, the sight of blood producing fantasies of castration and death. It is not unusual for a girl, especially if her mother has neglected to tell her in advance about menstruation, to imagine she is bleeding to death as punishment for all her "sins" (masturbation fantasies about marrying her father, fantasies about killing her mother and siblings).

Penis envy seems to appear in two distinct stages— "envy by the girl of the boy's possession of the special (one might say from the visual angle of the little girl), the *extra* organ, and envy of its special functional capacities, notably as an organ of urination and of masturbation," according to Dr. Phyllis Greenacre. She says penis envy is particularly strong in little girls between the ages of three to five, with perhaps the peak of envy occurring during the phallic phase when the girl-child becomes aware of the relative inadequacy of her "clitoral miniature," compared to the greater importance of the phallus.

"It has been my own observation," Greenacre continues, "that such awareness of difference [between a boy and a girl] becomes painful and the subject of envy, especially if the child has recently been subjected to other narcissistic blows and deprivations (such as illness, separation from the mother, loss of a playmate)." Fantasies of restitution, such as the belief a penis will grow later, or during the night, may occur, she states, adding "It seems that these theories gain special reality fortification from the concurrent experience of growing teeth and seeing vaguely the replacement of fingernails."

Greenacre differentiates between penis envy and penis awe, thus showing women may have several fantasies at this phase of development about the penis. She says penis awe occurs as the result of the observation by the small girl of the penis of an adult man, either in its flaccid state or as it moves into a state of erection. The age of the little girl when she first observes the penis will determine the persistence of her feeling of penis awe—the earlier she sees the adult penis, the more in awe of it she will generally feel.

In her envy of the penis, many a woman adorns herself with feathers, sequins, furs, glistening silver and gold ornaments that "hang down"—what psychoanalysts call "representations" of the penis. One reason large breasts are envied, by both men and women, is that in fantasy they represent the penis—a breast projects from the body, is an erogenous zone, and (in lactating women) ejects a fluid. In some primitive tribes, women bind their breasts so they protrude stiffly in front, like an erect penis. (Primitive man was very open in his worship of the phallus. During tribal ceremonies, the men carried false phalluses of enormous size, equating the phallus with power. Before setting forth to conquer an enemy, they held rites centering on phallic activities.) To a man, the sight of large breasts may allay his fear of castration. The large breast also, from fantasies of the oral stage, represents the generous, feeding mother. Men who cannot be sensual and tender toward a woman's breast, and women who cannot allow men such feelings toward their breasts, probably had feeding difficulties as infants.

To a woman who unconsciously seeks the coveted penis, a man may stand only for that organ and not as another human being. She considers the sexual part as the whole. The man in her fantasy becomes her appendage, enhancing her, making her feel strong and powerful. Some women feel they cannot appear socially without a man. "If I don't have a man by my side at cocktail parties, or at dinners, I feel worthless, a nobody," said one well-known actress. She showed off a man to other women as though he were her possession, her "thing"—a word sometimes used by men to describe their penises.

Marilyn Monroe, despite her glamorous appearance, was revealed in her husband Arthur Miller's play *After the Fall* as a clinging little girl who treated a man as though he were her possession, her substitute penis. This is understandable in view of the actress's early life, which included the trauma of separation from her mother and then a sexual seduction. Her excessive oral dependency, stemming from unfulfilled needs for a mother's love, was transferred to men when she grew older, and masqueraded as sexual seductiveness.

Dreams of many a woman after her first act of intercourse reveal "an unmistakable wish . . . to keep for herself the penis with which she had come in contact," Freud noted, remarking too that "these dreams indicated a temporary regression from the man to the penis as an object of desire."

One fantasy of the woman is that she can possess a penis by incorporating it orally—seizing it, biting it off and swallowing it, in the belief that "I now myself have become a penis," according to Dr. Otto Fenichel.

Fenichel describes the case of a woman in whose sexual life voyeurism played an important role, in whom "the wish to see a penis covered the deeper one of eating it. This oral-sadistic possessing of the 'seen' was meant as a genuine introjection and hence resulted also in identifications [with the male]." Such a fantasy stems from the infant's belief that he has only to swallow something and it becomes part of him.

Psychoanalysts often find in women simultaneously the fantasy of possessing a penis and of being one, according to Dr. Bertram Lewin. He explains that women identify themselves—their whole body—with a penis, "via the pathway of oral introjection." He gives as an example a woman who acted so completely subservient to a man that she gratified his every wish, as though she herself were a part of his body, the coveted part, the penis.

Some women, on the other hand, act as though they do not need a man. Their penis envy causes them to identify with men so completely that they act like men. The Amazons were prime examples.

Deborah Sampson was an example of a woman determined to play the role of a man, at least for a certain period of her life, out of deep patriotism for her country. This amazing woman, who might be called America's "first feminist," was born on December 17, 1760, in Plympton, Massachusetts. At the age of twenty-two, disguised as a man, she enlisted as a soldier in the Revolutionary War, and was stationed at West Point, where she served eighteen months until the war's end. She then married and had three children, so we may conclude that she conquered her Oedipal conflict enough to marry and bear children.

What he calls "the impossible wish," the desire of a little girl to completely possess her father, is described by Dr. Warren J. Gadpaille in his book *The Cycles of Sex*. He points out that from the age of three or four to about five or six, there comes a surge in childhood sexuality with deep implications for the child's future sexual life. Psychoanalysts call this period the "phallic stage," but this is in some ways a misnomer since it implies that female psychosexual development is subordinate to that of the male, Gadpaille says.

"The term is not entirely inaccurate, however, if one explores it without making value judgments, because, for a time, healthy as well as conflicted girls do adopt an unconsciously male stance in attempting to cope with their heightened sexuality," he explains. "The healthy ones move through and out of the 'phallic' position to a new and further stage of femininity that does not represent a compromise with inaccessible maleness. Those who are less well prepared emotionally have problems with their evolving identities."

The stage is called "phallic" because psychoanalysts universally have observed that genital sensations, fantasies, and drives for gratification reach a level of preoccupation in children of this age, most obvious in the intense concern of boys with their penises but, when looked for, scarcely less obvious among girls. Freud originated the term "phallic stage" out of his theory that the penis was the primary sexual organ in the minds of both boys and girls and that girls become feminine with great reluctance, only when forced to relinquish their phallic strivings. The term can be retained without subscribing to the male dominance theory, Gadpaille believes.

The child's sexual drive increases during the phallic stage and what the child, his parents, and his culture do about it largely determines the further development of the drive. According to Gadpaille, "The quality of earlier preparations and relationships and the attitudes toward childhood sex play strongly influence the child's response to the biologically intensified sexuality, and the biological influences enforce conditions requiring the child to learn more about growing up male or female."

During the phallic stage the Oedipus complex develops; the phallic stage ends when the conflicts inherent in the Oedipal situation are resolved and the genital, or final stage, is entered. The Oedipal situation, in which the child's genital sensations become focused upon the parent of the opposite sex, is normal, not pathological. "The Oedipus complex not only happens, it is essential for normal psychosexual development," Gadpaille comments. "It is only when something goes awry in coping with these normal feelings that emotional trouble develops."

The child now has an object for his heightened sexual urges and he begins to have masturbatory fantasies related to the parent of the opposite sex. This is sometimes verbalized in frank form, but most of the wishes and conflicts appear in the child's fantasies, including those that accompany masturbation, with resultant guilt.

To a little girl, her incestuous fantasies imply displacing and replacing her mother, and for these wishes she expects punishment. "The little girl ultimately wants to be daddy's love not along with, but instead of, mother," says Gadpaille. "Such fantasies cannot be entertained without the accompanying fears of potential retaliation" —for daring to intrude into the relationship between her parents.

At the phallic stage the imagined rivalry with the parent of the same sex and the enhanced pleasure value of the penis "combine to make castration a fantasy truly to be feared," Gadpaille notes, adding that children use fantasy both to imagine disguised gratification of their wishes—their hostile, murderous ones as well as their incestuous ones—and also to protect themselves from guilt.

There is both a "phallic" and a feminine component to the psychosexual development of girls when they reach this stage, Gadpaille states. Girls face a double dilemma since their principal and primary love, the mother, has been female, and they have to transfer it to someone with a different kind of body. The phallic stage achieves disturbing proportions only in those girls who are already beginning to find their femaleness difficult to accept, or for whom obstacles are provided at this time against assuming their feminine sexual identity, he says.

"Otherwise, the phallic stage of a girl and its accompanying burst of fairly intense penis envy becomes subordinated to her evolving primary femaleness," he asserts.

At this time the clitoris becomes the focus of intense erotic pleasure and produces, as a rule, a corresponding increase of clitoral masturbation. It is now, too, that the little girl realizes she cannot have a real baby despite her magical wish and is ready to repudiate this wish, repress it. The newly eroticized clitoris helps her to externalize her sexuality, the way boys are able to do through masturbation, rather than accept her sexual organs as chiefly hidden from sight. "Many girls, in the interest of externalization, repress the knowledge of the vaginal opening and deny awareness of its existence," Gadpaille comments.

The first source of a girl's envy of the penis may derive from the literalness of the child's mental processes— because the penis is bigger than her clitoris, it must therefore give more pleasure, the girl believes. The second source of her envy arises from her initial desire to focus her love on her mother, where it has always been. He explains, "Her sexual drive is now erotic, and in order to love her mother as her father does she needs a penis. It is more this *functional* wish than a belief that little boys are naturally superior that endows the penis with its temporarily supreme value."

When she realizes the impossibility of her phallic wishes, the little girl turns from her mother toward her father, in frustration and disappointment. Gadpaille asserts, "Now begins a crystallizing of the considerable ambivalence that characterizes the feelings of even the happiest and healthiest of little girls toward their mothers. Normally, the mother has been the source of far too much love and pleasure and caring for the little girl to cease loving her; but she is also the source of a myriad real and imaginary disappointments and dissatisfactions, all of which crowd together in the girl's emotions at this time."

Since the mother interfered with her pleasure by weaning her, toilet-training her, disciplining her, bringing rivals into the house in the form of brothers and sisters, seeming to be the most powerful figure in the home, it is the mother whom the little girl unconsciously blames for not having provided her with the penis she needs in order to love her mother as her father does. The little girl believes her mother obviously prefers her father as a sexual love object and that she "loses" her mother, her first love, because she lacks a particular body part, Gadpaille says.

In turning toward her father, the little girl is not impelled solely, or even primarily, by her disappointment over not being a penis-bearing male, but prompted largely by the normal facets of female identity and preferences that have been developing under the influence of her parents. "If her parents have been exemplifying and fostering an acceptance of rewarding heterosexual complementarity, her phallic interest in her mother will pass relatively quietly," Gadpaille continues. "Her sexual drives will turn naturally, not reluctantly and by default, toward her first and most logical heterosexual love object, her father."

As the phallic phase succumbs to what Gadpaille calls "the weight of reality," the little girl eventually represses her wish to have a penis and to sexually possess her mother and then her father.

"At this point, having met with frustration in both phallic and Oedipal strivings, a little girl has some realistic, though thoroughly misperceived reasons to feel temporarily inferior to everyone in her typical family," Gadpaille maintains. "Her mother has babies, breasts, and her father's love; her father has a large penis and her mother's sexual love; her brother has a penis which gives him a fantasy edge in winning her mother or a substitute, and his equipment more closely resembles her father's than hers resembles her mother's. Children of both sexes, but perhaps especially girls, need helpful and understanding parents to make sure that they garner the many benefits of this crucial stage and avoid its potential hazards."

Only through resolution of the Oedipal conflict does a child "take his first definitive step toward an integrated sexual identity," Gadpaille points out. The inevitable failure of his Oedipal fantasies leads to resignation, guilt, and anxiety, and the renunciation of "the impossible wish" is motivated in part, he says, by the need to relieve these unpleasant emotions as well as by the positive ties of love for the parent of the same sex, the pressure of innate forces toward healthy sexual identity, the growing power of reality over magical omnipotent thinking, and the influence of healthy sexual self-concepts inculcated by parents throughout childhood thus far.

Under the impetus of all these forces, the little girl

gives up rivalry with her mother and, instead, identifies with her, accepting the reality that one day she will grow up and find her own sexual partner. Thus she eases her guilt, fear, and anger and frees herself for growth in the final, or genital, stage of psychosexual development.

Most of us have difficulty remembering our Oedipal fantasies because virtually all memory of childhood sexuality, even of the first five or six years of life, is repressed. Freud said this universal childhood amnesia was caused by the high degree of anxiety produced by Oedipal feelings.

In contrast to the boy's Oedipus complex, resolved by castration anxiety (his fear of losing his penis if he sexually desires his mother), the girl's resolution of the Oedipus complex, Gadpaille points out, is said to be "brought on" by the fear of a fantasied castration or resentment over the fantasy that castration already has been accomplished. He maintains the validity of the comparison depends in part upon the intensity of the girl's phallic strivings and subsequent frustration.

"In those girls with strong penis envy, who resent bitterly their fantasied castration, it is accurate to say that they turn their sexual wishes toward their fathers in genuine disappointment over not being a boy," he explains. "In a girl whose femaleness has been positively reinforced throughout her earlier childhood, the phallic phase is less intense and she is less driven toward her father by castration anxiety than pulled toward him by developing heterosexual responsiveness. In order words, the Oedipal attachments of girls express strong components of natural and positive femininity, not merely reluctant compensations for not having been a boy."

He adds however that the fact that a little girl has no penis contributes to the slower and sometimes incomplete resolution of her Oedipal attachment to her father.

Resolution comes about more through disappointment by the father than through fear of the mother.

"The Oedipal period is the first crucial opportunity to learn to *like* being a girl," says Gadpaille. "The girl's sexual desire for her father includes pleasure in being his opposite, a female, but the impossibility of satisfying her desire and the disappointment and hurt at her failure can revive her shame over being a girl if this was a serious conflict at an earlier time. Her fantasied humiliation at being female may be such that identification with her mother is impossible and every aspect of femininity must be denied."

This may be a basis for "tomboyism," he says, of the persistent and defiant kind that so clearly signals rejection of femaleness. He comments, "Some girls become little 'toughs' in the effort to pretend to themselves that they are really boys, behaving as though they actually possess the coveted penis."

Gadpaille makes an interesting observation. He maintains that because girls do not have to fear the loss of a penis, part of their superego, or conscience, which derives its power from castration anxiety, is weaker than men's. "The rigid and persistently infantile quality of the male superego wreaks much interpersonal and social havoc," he states. "In order to keep themselves in line lest their dangerous impulses break through, men are much more likely than women to become authoritarian personalities, to reinforce their own repression by demanding that others hold the same values as they, and to feel threatened by differences. Males kill each other and make wars over the most trivial issues of 'honor' and national pride. . . . Clinical experiences and historical evidence suggests an admirable emotional flexibility in women with regard to reaching reasonable and humane adaptations to difficult situations. The probability that one contribution to female flexibility is a woman's less powerful childish superego suggests this may be an advantage, rather than the handicap it has frequently been labeled."

During prepuberty, between the ages of six and twelve, girls may experience a revival of the emotional disturbances and unresolved conflicts of infantile sexuality, according to Dr. Phyllis Greenacre. Such disturbances involve a "stubbornly intense effort to solve the castration problem through the persistence of the illusory penis," she says.

Psychoanalysts maintain there is much evidence that "primary disturbance," or conflict during oral development, is a very important factor in later sexual difficulties. The crippling of a child's psychosexual development begins with the hostility, either active or passive, of both mother and infant: too early or too late weaning, or the primal scene witnessed during the time of weaning, may cause acute oral frustration and rage in an infant.

The time in a child's life at which a trauma occurs is significant. One woman in analysis recalled she had received a severe spanking from her father at the age of two for wetting her bed at night (he later referred frequently to this with a sense of pride, claiming the spanking had "cured" her of bedwetting). This happened at the time of the birth of her younger brother. Her fantasy was that she was being spanked because she wished her new rival dead. Had the spanking taken place later, or earlier, possibly she would not have felt it as so traumatic.

There are many ways a parent can interfere with the natural psychosexual development of a little girl, causing her to remain too intensely in a fantasy world. One way is for a mother to give her enemas or to insert suppositories in the child's rectum, to allay her fear that the little girl will be constipated. Such a mother becomes the "phallic mother." The enema tube or suppository represents her phantom penis, penetrating one of the child's sexual orifices and creating terrifying fantasies in the little girl's mind as she wonders in horror, "What is mommy doing to me?" Her reactions will be both sexual and hostile.

Other ways in which parents may arouse a little girl sexually are by using obscene or sexually explicit language, acting out vicariously their sexual desires, or indulging in promiscuity, making no secret of this before the child. They also may appear nude in front of her continually, or allow her to witness or overhear them in sexual intercourse or prolonged foreplay. Dr. Henry Edelheit maintains that fantasies of crucifixions and similar themes, such as the bound Prometheus or Joan of Arc at the stake, are common in children who witness the primal scene and identify with both parents.

"In crucifixion fantasies the crucified Christ represents the parents locked or nailed together in intercourse and at the same time, by way of the double identification, the helpless observing child," he explains. The primal scene is interpreted as a sadistic act.

But imposed on this scene, he maintains, is a former image, that of the nursing mother and child. These combined images account, Edelheit says, "for the frequent oral or polymorphous elaboration of these fantasies. The regressive effect of the nursing impulse is also responsible, I believe, for the frequent occurrence in primal scene fantasies of androgynous, hybrid, and composite forms, representing fusions of man and woman, mouth and breast, mother and child."

Our sexuality is the result of a developmental process that starts at birth, possibly in the womb. The phase called "polymorphous perverse" occurs before genital primacy has been achieved. It contains the drives of both the oral and anal phases which, in the genital stage, are drawn together and dominated by the powerful genital urge. Freud compared the oral and anal drives to tributaries leading into "the great river of genitality."

He also pointed out that as a woman transfers her erotic love from her mother to her father, there is a change in the nature of her aims. She wants a man not to nurse her as her mother did but to protect her, think her lovely and desirable. This is part of what Freud called "the transformation of the instinct." A woman, for instance, has the wish to have a penis which then "undergoes transformation" as it becomes the wish to have a baby.

The mature woman is dominated by her genital impulses. She has given up her desire to be a man. This does not mean she will not seek a career or try to win a place in a man's world. There is a great difference between the woman driven by a desperate unconscious wish to be a man and one who chooses to pursue goals usually associated with masculine achievements because she wishes greater self-realization. The driven woman holds men in contempt, even as she competes with them. It is impossible for a woman to be a friend to a man with whom she is sexually involved if she feels hatred for him because of her unconscious envy. Friendship is an important part of lasting relationships between the sexes: passionate love soon loses its intensity, and unless respect and friendship remain, a relationship may be doomed.

Whether a girl grows up wishing to be a man or is comfortable about her femininity is probably determined for the most part by the feelings that exist between her and her mother. If her hatred outweighs her love, she will hate being a woman.

If a mother is unhappy, depressed, complaining, unable to hold a husband, her daughter thinks, "Why should I want to be like *her*—a woman?" If the daughter is contemptuous of the feminine model offered by her mother she will choose in fantasy to be a man. She may become asexual, lesbian, or promiscuous, refusing to accept any one man as mate, or she may undertake a number of marriages, all unsuccessful.

The dissatisfaction with and hatred of the mother starts in infancy. If the mother consciously or unconsciously has not wanted a baby, this will communicate itself to the infant. Probably the most intolerable conviction a child bears is of not being wanted, as Dr. Gregory Rochlin points out in his book, *Griefs and Discontents, The Forces of Change.* He explains: "It is an oppressive and alarming belief. It makes the child feel worthless and sink in his self-esteem—the sense of loss—and it arouses in him the anxiety that he must fend for himself and cannot expect favor or fortune. In the struggle against his distress he develops special and characteristic emotional reactions as defenses. He may depend upon denial: supporting his vanity by grandiose and extravagant fantasies that assert the opposite of what he feels to be true and make him feel worthy and important."

The mother may be particularly unhappy at having borne a "girl" and this too the baby girl will feel, and then hate herself for being feminine. In general, the very disturbed mother who has little self-esteem cannot pass on a sense of self-esteem to her daughter and therefore cripples her psychosexual development.

Every girl is somewhat ambivalent about her mother, but an excessively hostile attitude creates fear of her mother's revenge as the girl projects her own hostility onto her mother. This anger and fear lead girls to curb their feminine identification: angry little girls do not wish to be feminine.

Abraham noted that mothers influence the psychosexual development of their daughters "either by speaking disparagingly of female sexuality to them, or by unconsciously giving them indications of their aversion to the man. The latter method is the more permanently effective one, because it tends to undermine the hetero-sexuality of the growing-up girl." And, adds Rochlin, a mother "establishes a girl's femininity during the first three years of the girl's life. What she wants her daughter to be to her determines her daughter's feelings about her own femaleness."

How a mother touches her baby girl's body—whether with love and gentleness or with fear and disgust—influences how the little girl will feel about her mother, as well as about her own body. One woman realized, during her analysis, that because her mother had always withdrawn from physical contact—a peremptory peck on the cheek was the only touch her mother allowed—she had feared the tender touch, either to give or receive it.

Psychoanalysts also stress the importance of the father in helping his little girl feel feminine and pretty so she will wish to grow up a woman. Fathers who remain aloof out of fear of emotional contact with their daughters, or who are excessively seductive, thereby arousing the little girl's fear of her own incestuous urges, interfere with the little girl's desire to accept her incipient woman-liness. Moreover, if a father downgrades the mother, the little girl will not wish to emulate her.

Emotional strains and hostilities between husbands and wives, when too frequently and too openly displayed before their children, have destructive effects. Many a little girl grows up believing her mother and father never had sexual relations except for the time she was con-ceived, because she has seen little or no affection ex-pressed between them. This enhances her own strong Oedipal wish to separate her parents sexually. In order to feel feminine, a woman must finally acknowledge that there was an ongoing sexual relationship between her mother and father—one from which she was necessarily excluded.

What makes it possible for one woman to accept her childhood wishes and fantasies and another woman not? Psychoanalysts say this depends on the woman's relative ego strength which, in the words of Dr. Walter Stewart, implies "distance from conflict."

Healthy ego strength enables a woman to withstand frustration and not to feel overwhelmed when she is insulted or rejected. It also enables her at certain times, such as during sexual intercourse, to permit herself to regress to a momentary loss of control that to a woman with a weak ego would be equated with castration fear or death.

The outcome of each woman's life will differ, depending on her early emotional experiences and her degree of trust in her parents. What constitutes a traumatic experience for one little girl will not emotionally devastate another, who has grown up with more love than hate in her home. As psychoanalysts point out, it is not so much the "natural" traumas—weaning, toilet training, the birth of a brother or sister, a temporary separation from the mother—that cause emotional conflicts, but the day-to-day living with parents who pass on to the child their own emotional disturbances. They make a little girl doubt their pleasure in her existence, undermine her self-esteem, and create in the home an aura of distrust and anger.

Paradoxically, overindulgence can prove as detrimental to the child's psychosexual development as harsh and restrictive parental attitudes. Sara Harris, who wrote *Cast the First Stone* and *Father Divine*, among other books, recalls, "My father always made me feel like a little princess. I was more important to him than his wives. He had no respect for women—except me." She paid a high price, she says, for such love: "My father's adoration made life harder eventually. I was never able to face my hatred for him. Nor was I able to tolerate frustration. My therapist once told me, 'Your problem is that frustration for you is impossible.' And it has been difficult to accept feelings of frustration, which inevitably occur as part of life."

The psychosexual development of women is no simple matter. If it were, there would be no perversions, no difficulty achieving heterosexuality. When emotional trauma in the oral, anal, and phallic stages has not been too damaging, a girl will not fear being a woman, or look on "woman" as inferior. She will not be afraid of being sexually penetrated by a man she loves. She will be receptive to him, though not submissive (an attitude concealing rage). Rather than angrily competing with men, the woman secure in her femininity will quietly seek equality with them. She will not need to throw herself frantically into a career in order to prove herself as good as if not better than a man. If she makes the choice of career, she does so with the knowledge that the more ways in which she fulfills herself, the richer her life will be.

Chapter 5

HELL HATH NO FURY—

It is easy to understand how the sexual desires of a woman may be repressed, then expressed in fantasies of love and sensuality. But the wishes and fantasies emerging from her other strong instinct—aggression—are not so apparent. Because throughout the centuries woman has had to deny her rage even more than her sexuality. Unlike the Duchess in *Alice in Wonderland,* who ordered "Off with his head!" whenever someone offended her, a woman has had to pretend she feels no anger in order to exist in comparative safety in the outside world.

"I had always been in a rage. I had been very angry since childhood. But what man would want an angry woman? The rage came out as charm." These words were spoken by Delphine Seyrig, the French actress appearing in the film "Last Year at Marienbad," in an interview published in The New York Times on July 31, 1976. They echo the sentiments of countless women.

Excessive charm, compliance, and politeness may be defenses used to cover a seething anger that will usually reveal itself in intimate situations.

One woman of thirty-nine told her analyst she prided herself on being a sweet, unselfish human being who never raised her voice in anger, or objected to anything her friends said or did, no matter how spiteful. "My reward is that everyone says I don't have an enemy in the world, everyone loves me."

Then she added, as tears came to her eyes, "But I feel miserable all the time."

"Why?" asked the analyst.

"For one thing, I don't believe them," she said. "For another, all the praise they give doesn't make me feel loved."

She eventually understood how her defense of sweetness and light hid deep feelings of anger that were dismissed from her consciousness whenever they arose. Through analysis she became less afraid of those feelings and more capable of expressing anger directly. She found she had a new sense of self-esteem.

Laughter has long been another defense against anger. In the play *Luv*, by Murray Shisgal, Eli Wallach, in the role of husband, shouts to his wife, played by Anne Jackson, after they have failed in an attempt to hurl his rival into the Hudson River, "I ask you to help me to do one simple, lousy little thing—murder!" This line brings down the house. The thought of murder as "a simple, lousy little thing" delights us all, giving release to our unconscious wish to kill off our rivals.

A woman is apt to go through a typical day, even if she does not step outside the house, with some murderous feelings and fantasies, for hatred is as much a part of life as love. Even toward those she loves, she will occasionally harbor murderous wishes, especially when they hurt her, which they are bound to do. She may envy the success of friends, or take pleasure in hearing about someone's misfortune, especially someone richer or more popular than she.

"I plan the most diabolical revenge on my arrogant, chauvinistic boss, as I stand in a jammed subway, body to body, on my way to work," says a young woman who is a Wall Street broker. "Usually I dream of putting arsenic in one of those lethal martinis he drinks at lunch. Or loosening the brakes on his Lincoln convertible so he will plunge off the George Washington Bridge as he drives home to his mansion in Englewood Heights—he lives in Jersey, of course, to escape the high New York State taxes."

In reading murder mystery novels, in watching murder movies on television, and in following real murders reported in the daily newspapers, a woman betrays her hidden wish to kill those who hurt her, as she participates vicariously in committing each murder. Unconsciously she does not want the murderer caught because she herself would like to get away with murder. It is interesting that two of the most popular mystery writers of all time are women—Agatha Christie and Josephine Tey.

Sometimes the wish to murder is not very deeply hidden. One wife could not stop herself from getting furious at her husband when he did something to annoy her, and it seemed almost everything about him annoyed her —the color of the suits he bought, his table manners, the way he combed his hair, the tone of his voice.

"Someday I am going to kill him," she told her analyst in a matter-of-fact voice. "I just won't be able to stand him any longer."

"Why don't you leave him?" the analyst asked.

She sighed. "I know he can't be as horrible as I think he is. What's the matter with me?"

"You are so angry you can't possibly see your husband as a human being," the analyst said.

"Why am I so full of anger?" she wondered.

It took months for her to explore her feelings about her husband, and also about her mother and father, before she understood why she was so angry. She was the daughter of a very depressed mother, a woman who never allowed herself to feel anger, and a violent father, who exploded in fury at the slightest provocation. She had imitated her mother, never daring to open her mouth in opposition to her father. She had chosen a mate whose mannerisms and tone of voice reminded her of her father. She could thereby permit herself to express anger at her husband as an outlet for her repressed anger at her father.

Hate holds in it the wish to kill and the desire for revenge. If a woman has strong fantasies of revenge on a mother or father, the fantasies keep her from being able to love a man. She is ruled by her anger, which stifles loving impulses that may rise to consciousness.

Sometimes a woman feels her anger is justified, that she is married to a dominating, selfish, infantile man. But then she must ask herself why she chose such a man. Like the woman above, she may unconsciously have selected him as an outlet for her repressed anger at parents and siblings.

A woman complained to friends that her boss was persecuting her. One friend asked other employees at the office about this man and learned he was, in reality, thoughtful and considerate of his staff. The woman was in fact displacing childhood feelings about her father onto her employer. She had felt, as a little girl, that her father was "persecuting" her when he asked her to do chores around the house and forbade her to go out with certain boys. Her fantasy of revenge on her father contained a tabooed wish (one should honor one's mother and father, not hate them), and so she indulged in the psychological process called projection. Her desire for revenge became more bearable as long as she could blame someone else— her boss—for her own dangerous wish.

A woman's hidden anger is often masked by depression. The depressed woman conceals from her own awareness the wish for revenge on someone who has hurt her. A psychoanalyst's main task with women who are depressed is to enable them to feel free enough to experience anger. Whether their anger is justified is not important: they must realize they are entitled to *feel* anger— an emotion so many little girls are required to repress when parents order them to be "nice" and "ladylike." (Little boys, who are expected to be more untractable and more violent than girls, have somewhat greater freedom in expressing their emotions.)

Coping with primitive desires occupies much of the early life of a little girl. When she loves her mother and father, she imagines them as gods. When she feels angry, they turn into devils. The belief that the father is all-powerful—sees, hears, and knows everything the infant thinks and feels—has produced the fantasy of God, according to Freud. "God" represents the good parent of infancy, the one who protects and gives orders that are beneficent. God is perfect and can do no wrong; to ally oneself with God means one is also perfect. The "devil", or the bad, frustrating parent, is based on another fantasy of infancy, according to Freud, who adds that the devil's horns represent displaced penises.

One outlet for the little girl's feelings of hatred is the fairy tale, which abounds in themes of murder and violence as well as love and romance. There is the hatred of siblings and the wicked stepmother in *Cinderella*, the killing of the giant in *Jack and the Beanstalk*, the roasting of the wicked witch in *Hansel and Gretel*, and the shooting of the big, bad wolf in *Red Riding Hood*.

That women may wish to kill is shown in the large number who actually *do* so, including their children. The battered and murdered child is sometimes attacked by his mother. Psychoanalysts say that such a woman, in her unconscious, is killing a part of herself she feels to be evil, as well as eliminating hated siblings. At least 10,000 children are beaten and seriously injured each year by mothers (and fathers as well),according to the Children's Division of the American Humane Association. Physical assaults on children by parents may even be a more frequent cause of death than serious childhood diseases.

One effect of the women's liberation movement appears to be that more women are acting out murderous fantasies and starting to equal men not only in the open expression of sexual desire but of hostile feelings as well. An increasing number of women are committing criminal acts, and their crimes are of a more violent nature. Women most often kill their infants, husbands, or lovers. Two attempted to assassinate Gerald Ford when he was President of the United States. In the California massacres led by Charles Manson, several young women committed bloody, savage acts of murder.

Major crime among women has increased more rapidly than among men not only because women are leaving the home to take part in industrial and social life (which includes more open drinking), but because the protective function of femininity needed to guard the newborn is no longer necessary, according to Dr. Lawrence Friedman. He cites the widespread use of contraceptives and the declining birth rate.

"The masculine part of the ambivalent struggle has become stronger in women and they have increasingly become more violent," says Friedman. He adds however that there is another, more constructive side to the picture: women are also using their "greater aggressivity for all kinds of purposes—one of them being a substitute for giving birth—the artistic creation. We are seeing an increasingly larger number of women produce most valuable artistic creations. The ability to do so was always there, but the need was lacking to the extent it exists today."

There is a difference between a society which permits women the freedom to feel anger that is justifiable and one which encourages a permissiveness that leads to violent acts. Discussing this difference, Dr. Martin Grotjahn explains that freedom is never bestowed on anyone but emanates from an inner feeling of self-esteem and self-confidence. Whereas permissiveness sanctions the demand for instant gratification—which, if frustrated, may lead to violence. Grotjahn points out that today's permissiveness encourages women to seek direct expression of their violent feelings.

A violent act is seldom without symbolic sexual meaning. Aggression, when it contains the guilt of infant sexual fantasies, may become sexualized, according to psychoanalysts. Similarly, the sexual act becomes "aggressivized" in rape or murder. In a severely emotionally disturbed man or woman, the sexual and aggressive drives are fused as they are in infancy.

At first Freud thought the sexual urge, concerned with procreation, was the only powerful human impulse. Later he theorized that the aggressive drive, concerned with self-preservation, was equally strong. When we feel in danger, actual or imagined, physical or psychic, all our energy automatically goes into saving our lives. If a little girl feels endangered by angry, cruel parents, her desire to save her life is stronger than her sexual drive. Her natural, erotic desires will therefore become crippled because of her intense need for revenge on parents who have not protected and guided her.

The manner in which a child is brought up and its effect on his later personality has been dramatically portrayed by Margaret Mead in her book *Sex and Temperament in Three Primitive Societies.* She describes the great differences between the Arapesh—a placid, nonviolent people of New Guinea—and their neighbors—the headhunting, cannibalistic Mundugumors.

The Arapesh baby is never left alone by its mother. If it cries, it is comforted at once. The Arapesh children grow up to be gentle and cooperative. The Mundugumors, on the other hand, raise their children in harshness and cruelty. When a baby cries, it is not fed promptly; it is neither cuddled nor made comfortable. Parents slap their children violently, often for disobeying a long list of "don'ts." These children, nurtured in anger, grow into savage adults.

When parents are cruel, cannot provide security and love, the primitive passions within a child become intensified by the parents' acts and fantasies, for the child imitates and carries out the wishes of his role models. The psychological study of a fourteen-year-old girl who murdered her father showed she was fulfilling the wishes of her mother, who openly hated her husband, wishing him dead for years. The girl's hatred of her father, a brutal man who beat her and her mother, was inflamed by her mother's daily rage.

What makes the difference between someone who merely fantasizes murder and someone who actually kills? Psychoanalytic studies show that, in a general sense, the amount of violence, actual and implied, experienced by a child at the hands of his mother and father (or whoever else brings him up) makes the difference. If a child feels loved, his normal fantasies of revenge are easily handled and sublimated, not needing to explode into murder. But when parents are brutal—physically or psychologically or both—and the child continually feels rejected, unwanted, and abused, his murderous fantasies are likely one day to overpower his conscious control.

A number of psychoanalysts have written of the effect of the unconscious, unspoken, criminal wishes of parents upon the behavior of children. Several have pointed out that in the legend of Oedipus, the tragic act was originally set in motion by the parents themselves, who ordered the infant Oedipus killed to prevent the prophecy of the Delphic oracle from coming true—that he would grow up to kill his father and marry his mother.

Dr. Hyman Spotnitz, who has written extensively about schizophrenia, states that if a mother encourages her child to express violence and rage, the child may later turn to crime, having her tacit approval to do so. Whereas if she punishes her child for expressing anger, the child, if his rage is intense, turns inward his murderous feelings for her and instead becomes schizophrenic. Excessive guilt over such feelings induces mental illness, which is a form of self-punishment, he observes.

Fantasies of childhood revenge underlie every murder. In his unconscious, the adult murderer is taking revenge on the cruel mother and father of childhood, no matter who the victim. Sometimes the victim *is* the original target of hatred, as when sons or daughters kill a parent. The case of Lizzie Borden from Fall River, Massachusetts, which occurred in 1892, has held such fascination over the years because it appears to be direct acting out of the Electra conflict (the feminine version of the Oedipus complex, named after the Greek heroine who murdered her mother in the hope of gaining her father's love).

From the facts known about Lizzie Borden, it seems evident she had never overcome her passionate girlhood attachment to her father. She considered him her possession, especially after her mother died. He colluded in maintaining this fantasy by giving his daughter his wedding ring, as though symbolically selecting her as his next bride. When he remarried, however, Lizzie's feelings of rejection, betrayal, and jealousy must have been overwhelming. She managed to conceal her rage until one hot summer day when they erupted in a rampage that culminated in the murder of her father and her rival stepmother. The murders may have occurred at this specific time because her father was about to change his will and leave most of his estate to his second wife, thus cutting Lizzie out of his life even further.

The deep hatred between siblings is another recurrent theme in ancient myths, the Biblical story of Cain and Abel perhaps the most famous example. If ever Freud's point needed to be proved—that in the unconscious part of his mind every murderer is killing one or all members of his childhood family—the modern-day case of Richard Speck did so. In Chicago in July of 1966, Speck murdered eight student nurses. There were eight persons in his childhood whom he must have hated—two brothers, four sisters, his mother, and his stepfather. The eight nurses symbolically represented the slaughter of Speck's family.

The question is asked how David Berkowitz, the alleged murderer known as "Son of Sam," could have been prevented from killing. Perhaps if earlier in life he had been able to express his deep hatred for the mother who bore him illegitimately and then gave him up, for the legitimate daughter she later had, for the father who never claimed him, and for the foster parents who had a daughter of their own (once again making him the "outcast"). On the very deepest level, as he shot at couples making love in parked cars, he may have had the fantasy that he was killing his mother and father in the sexual act which culminated in his own conception and subsequent abandonment.

Fantasies of revenge begin in the crib, perhaps even in the mother's uterus. Freud said that the seeds of war were to be found in the nursery. A baby girl's way of thinking about the world is through her mouth during the first, or oral stage, of psychosexual development. In her fantasies of revenge, she swallows, chews to pieces, and devours her victim. She is a little cannibal. As she learns to control her excretory functions, in the anal stage, her technique of murder becomes refined a bit as she fantasies revenge in terms of "peeing on" and "shitting on" her oppressors. In the third, or phallic state, she imagines she has a penis to use as weapon, which is what the promiscuous woman does in using sex to punish a man—"hitting and running" sexually, so to speak. In her fantasies her clitoris may be her "little penis", or during the sexual act she may identify with the man.

A common way of expressing hatred is through the use of obscene words. Words related to excretory functions or sexual activity, when used to show contempt and hostility, indicate the close connection between sexual and aggressive fantasies.

The major obscene word today is not "fuck" but one far more meaningful in our early life, according to Dr. Leo Stone. Tracing the history of the word "fuck" and its appearance in literature and dictionaries, Dr. Stone, in an article, "On the Principal Obscene Word in the English Language," concluded that the word "suck" was more obscene. He points out the similarity in "unconscious rhyme relation" of the "heretofore taboo word "fuck'" and the word "suck." He suggests the "pleasure and often guilty excitement" which accompanies the use of the word "fuck" is displaced onto it from the earlier, far more taboo process of "sucking," associated unconsciously with the mother who once was "sucked." He comments, "This would not be too surprising, insofar as it is sucking and suckling that distinguish the entire vertebrate class to which we belong."

Little girls, until they are taught to control anger, show no difficulty admitting murderous wishes. It is not unusual to hear a little girl say of a new sibling, especially if it is a boy, "Take it away. I don't want it in the house." Or she will hit the new baby in its crib. Or sadly stand beside it, in despair at having lost her mother's undivided love.

A six-year-old girl said to her mother just after she had given birth to a son, "I hate you! You're not my real mother." Then she threatened, "I'll go out in the snow without any clothes and get pneumonia and die and then you'll be sorry." She felt a helpless rage at this giantess who had the power of life and death over her and had just betrayed her by producing a new baby. She wanted to kill her mother, but instead directed the rage at herself—choosing suicide in her conscious fantasy.

One articulate little girl with reading problems unashamedly fantasied almost every possible death as the fate of her loved-hated objects. She informed her therapist, "When my mother tells me to do something I don't want to do, like button my sweater or comb my hair, I imagine her boiling on the stove in a big pot. Or dying of scarlet fever and taken to heaven by the angels. Or murdered by a robber who steals into our house while I am out playing."

She said of her father: "And when he won't take me with him on his boat or to the golf course, I imagine him falling off the boat and swallowed by sharks. Or dying of too much sun on the golf course. Or poisoned by bad hamburgers when he lunches with his boss."

Of her older brother: "When Brian steals my doll and marks up her face with red paint, I imagine him kidnapped and strangled by his kidnappers. Or stoned to death by his baseball team for striking out. Or starved to death by my mother because she caught him stealing a dollar from her pocketbook."

Of her second-grade teacher: "When Miss Marsh scolds me for talking to my friends in class, I imagine her thrown out in the snow by the principal because she came to school late, where she freezes to death. Or chokes to death from eraser dust. Or dies of a broken heart because her boy friend left her."

Of her best friend: "When Georgina insists on going to the zoo even though she knows I want to go to the movies, I imagine her dying after stuffing herself with chocolate cake at the supper table. Or eaten alive by the alligator at the zoo when she steps too near the river in which he is swimming. Or burned to death when her house catches fire from a cigarette ash that fell on the floor as her mother was smoking."

One reason women repress angry feelings is their fear, carried from childhood, of punishment for such feelings. This fear may be seen in persons afraid to fly because they think their airplane will crash, even though statistics show the air lanes to be safer than highways.

One woman, discussing her fear of planes, said to her analyst, "From the moment I walk out of my apartment and step into a taxi for La Guardia Airport or Kennedy, I feel I am on my way to death."

"Leaving your home means death to you," he said.

"It always did. When I was little and wanted to go down the street and play with friends, my mother wouldn't let me. She insisted I stay in the yard. She made me feel that to leave her would be the end of me."

"Did she threaten to punish you if you left the yard?"

"She sure did. Once I disobeyed her and went next door. She spanked me hard. I can still feel it."

"No wonder you feel guilty when you start off on a trip," the analyst said. "It revives those earlier memories."

"It isn't only the fear of flying that scares me?"

"It's the fear of separating from your mother and the punishment you will receive."

The overprotective mother is often concealing hostile wishes. Her conscious fantasy is that some danger will befall the little girl as she warns, "Look out for cars as you cross the street—don't get killed!" Or, "Put on your raincoat and rubbers or you'll catch your death of cold." But her unconscious fantasy, projected onto some external danger, is that *she* may harm the child. Dr. Sandor Rado says that mothers, when experiencing their baby as a frustration, will respond with rage and if the love grows weaker and the rage grows stronger "neglectful maternal behavior results, with consequences to the baby." But if "love prevails over rage, and the rage is suppressed for the sake of love, the result is the typical overcompensatory behavior that tends toward overprotection. In order to keep that anger in check, her love is overdone. It is as if the overprotective mother were trying to protect the child against her own hostility. The pattern is overcompensatory love and, underneath that, hatred."

Parents arouse anger in a little girl when they "mock" her or laugh at her for what she considers "important"—which to a parent may seem trivial. This is a form of brutality, for the "cutting" word is interpreted by the little girl as a mutilation of her body. As Freud pointed out, our first ego is a "body ego" and when someone injures our self-esteem, we unconsciously experience it as physical injury. Why parents do not think a child has self-esteem is one of the mysteries of life. Perhaps because their own parents never treated them with respect and so they unconsciously perpetuate the psychic sins of the past by repeating them with their children.

The violent fantasies of some women lie hidden in their phobias, which—as Freud discovered—serve to defend against both destructive and sexual impulses. A phobia is a reaction to the threat of an inner wish regarded as dangerous to the self.

One woman could not leave anything with a sharp point exposed in her apartment at night. She would hide scissors lying on her bureau in a drawer. She would put away all knives in the kitchen. Of what was she afraid? That she would get up in the middle of the night and harm herself, or someone else. Or that someone might break into her apartment, seize the visible knife or scissors, and attack her as punishment for her hostile thoughts.

Xenophobia is a somewhat subtler phobic reaction. There is in all of us a primitive antipathy toward "the stranger," anyone who differs from us in any way, but especially those whose bodies are different—which may be one reason for the unconscious war between the sexes. Some women openly wish, and feel they deserve, revenge on the men who over the years have deprived them of their rights. A few leaders of the women's liberation movement are as sexist as they accuse men of being. They do not look on a man as a partner but an enemy. They kill not with the sword but the word. The very phrase "male chauvinist pig" tells as much about the women who use it as the men at whom it is hurled.

Some women feel especially angry during the menstrual period. Not only do they have their inner feelings to contend with—that the monthly bleeding represents castration, makes them feel dirty, inferior, maimed—but society's attitude as well. In some primitive tribes menstruating women were kept secluded so they would not "spoil" the crops, the hunting and fishing, or the successful waging of war. Young girls at their first menstrual period were banished for three years to solitary confinement by some tribes, according to a recent book, *The Curse: A Cultural History of Menstruation* by Janice Delaney, Mary Jane Lupton, and Emily Toth.

A special kind of anger ensues when someone we love deserts us, an anger containing grief and despair. Rejection by a loved one can cause deep depression, or provoke suicide or murder. Dr. Emanuel Tanay, author of *The Murderers,* points out that many murders take place because a loved one threatens to leave. To feel rejected carries with it the wish to kill the one who is causing us such pain. Tanay reports that at least seventy percent of murders in the United States are committed against someone "near and dear." In Chicago in 1965, out of a total of 395 persons killed, 31 were husbands murdered by wives and 45 were wives killed by husbands. Only seven were gangland murders.

If a loved one dies of natural causes or in an accident, this is also felt as rejection by those left behind. In extreme cases the mourner, caught in his ambivalent feelings, may kill himself slowly through drinking or physical illness, or swiftly, in an accident or suicide. On one level the mourner is expressing the desire to rejoin the loved one in death. Studies of widowers who have been healthy show they die soon after their wives in larger numbers than men of the same age who are married or single.

It is in her dreams a woman may find expression of her deep hostile feelings. The dream is an escape valve for her repressed love and hate urges. Dreams contain the wishes of childhood buried because of social taboos: Thou shalt not kill. Thou shalt not covet thy neighbor's wife. Thou shalt not steal. Thou shalt not tell a lie.

Nightmares, which ancient man ascribed to "evil spirits" entering the body, reflect our most terrifying fears and wishes. When we wake up screaming from a nightmare, the emotion felt in the dream has become too dangerous for the dream to continue. We have had, for the moment, too stark a look into our unconscious.

The story of a dream, what Freud called its "manifest content," is never what it seems—otherwise there would be no need to dream. If we consciously knew what troubled us, repression would not exist. To discover a dream's hidden fantasies, what Freud called its "latent content," the mind must wander freely in connection with each of the dream's details, uncovering memories and wishes of the past that in some way still disturb us.

One woman dreamed she was chased by gangsters. They caught her, locked her in a room on the second floor of a lonely farmhouse, and threatened to kill her if she tried to escape. She threw a sheet over the window sill, intending to slide down. The door suddenly opened and a man resembling Clint Eastwood approached her, knife in hand. As he was about to plunge it into her, she woke screaming.

In telling this dream to her analyst, the woman mentioned that her husband looked like Clint Eastwood. She said, "Just before I fell asleep, my husband wanted sex. I didn't feel like it. But I was afraid to say no because I knew he would get angry. He doesn't like to be rejected in bed. So he had his orgasm. I didn't even try to have one, I felt so numb."

The dream shows she thinks of men as gangsters from whom she tries to escape, and of sex as a violent assault.

In her unconscious, a man's penis penetrating her is comparable to his plunging a knife into her. The dream not only mirrors her fear of sex but also shows a hidden hostile wish turned inward. She felt like killing her husband because he forced sexual intimacy on her. Since dreams often use reversals, in this instance the would-be killer (the dreamer) is portrayed as victim. The sheet in the dream, by which she hopes to escape, represents the sheet on her bed with which she wished to cover herself and escape the torment of unfulfilled sex with her husband.

One woman told her analyst of a dream in which she picked up a stranger at a singles bar. She invited him to her apartment and they had intercourse. A few weeks later she discovered she was pregnant by the strange man, whom she did not know how to locate. She woke in tears, thinking, I'll have to get an abortion, I can't have a baby without a father on the scene.

As she related the dream, she mentioned the stranger was wearing a long red and green plaid coat, adding in surprise, "Like Sherlock Holmes!" Then she said, "My father once had a coat like that. We teased him about his cloak of many colors. He adored that coat, wore it until it fell off his back in shreds." She also recalled that her father, Sherman, was nicknamed "Sher"—further identification of him as the stranger in her dream, whom she had said resembled "Sher"-lock Holmes.

The dream showed her wish to have a baby by her father—the natural wish of every little girl—which she repressed as she grew up. The intensity of the wish, and the conflict about it, remained out of her awareness, appearing only in her dream.

Dreams show that when rational controls are lifted, a hidden world of feelings and memories fleetingly dominate our lives. It is a world we reject or ignore as nonsensical, crazy, or obscene when we wake: "I would never think of such a thing in my wildest dreams," we often say. Yet, as Dr. Walter Stewart points out, it is *exactly* in our dreams that our most deeply buried wishes appear.

"The dream is the unique normal experience which allows us to open a closed door to greater self-understanding," Stewart says. "Dreams offer a route to insight about ourselves not available any other way." If we understand a dream we can bring past and present together. This enables us to understand conflicts that have remained unmastered and unresolved. We can free ourselves from endless repetition of stereotyped, destructive behavior that may be governing our lives.

Stewart explains: "Dreams provide a second chance to settle the unfinished business of life because they can bring back the crucial but repressed experiences which deform our characters and limit our responses. If we take our dreams seriously we can face aspects of ourselves we have chosen to forget."

One woman told her analyst of a dream in which she and her seven-year-old daughter were fleeing "a drunken stranger" through what she described as "a black forest." Suddenly she stopped in her flight, turned on the stranger. She grabbed him by the throat, squeezed it so violently that blood and entrails gushed out of his body in a black stream, leaving only skin and bones. She woke horrified.

"How could I possibly do that to a man?" she asked. "And who was the man?"

"You refer to him as a drunken stranger," said the analyst. "Was there anything familiar about him?"

"No," she said emphatically.

"What man in your life drank a lot?" the analyst asked.

"My father," she admitted.

"Do you remember any time your father chased you while he was drunk?"

She thought for a moment, then said, "When I was fifteen, I got all dressed up for the junior prom. I came down the stairs in my first grownup party dress—black crepe with shoulder straps of rhinestones. I felt like a princess. My father, who was quite drunk, ordered me upstairs. He said I looked too sophisticated for my age and should take off the black dress and put on my old blue taffeta. I refused. He started chasing me around the living room. He caught up with me and tore one of the shoulder straps. I burst into tears and ran upstairs, shrieking that I wasn't going to the prom. My mother sewed the strap back on, told me my father didn't mean what he said. Then she helped me sneak out of the house through the kitchen door so he wouldn't see me in the black dress. The next day he had forgotten all about it."

"But you didn't forget. You have been repressing fury at your father, who chased you, like the stranger did in your dream," said the analyst. "You have wanted to kill your father, choke every bit of blood and guts out of his body for what he did to you."

The "black forest" represented her black dress, the "blackness" covering the "forest," symbol of her pubic hair. Her father had been saying he thought she looked too sexy in the dress and she had understood his real accusation.

"I could never admit anger at my father," she said.

"It's dangerous to defy a drunken man—he might kill you," said the analyst. "You had to repress your 'black rage.'"

He asked what she had done, or thought, or seen the day before that might have stirred the memory portrayed in the dream. She said, without hesitating, "I stood for a long time in front of a window at Bonwit Teller's staring mesmerized at a black dress with a rhinestone collar." The sight of that black dress awoke memories of the earlier black dress in her life, one that had caused torment and a rage she had to deny.

Several psychoanalysts have noted that since the women's liberation movement, women patients reveal more dreams containing hostile fantasies. As women feel more entitled to acknowledge anger, it finds freer expression in dreams. Joseph Katz, in his recent book *Dreams Are Your Truest Friends,* says, "Women's dreams are clearly changing, becoming less submissive, and there is less acting the role of the helpless, fearful victim destined to suffer endless humiliation with its inevitable build-up of anger."

Contemporary woman, having gained considerable sexual freedom, may be overemphasizing and overevaluating the power, importance, and joy of sexual activity, says Dr. Martin Grotjahn. But he notes that never before "have I heard so many women so frequently complain about sexual apathy of the male than in the last five years. It seems as if males are taking the lead in the direction of a kind of sexual apathy, a lack of interest, a quiescence, aiming at a behavior somewhat like the time before the sexual revolution started, but for different reasons. While women are in the forefront of sexual discovery, the male, spoiled by easy success, settles down—not to enjoy the prize of victory but perhaps to enjoy a rest. The 'cool'generation is taking over. Passion may be out of style. Playboys replace the lover."

Do men feel an increasing impotence because of woman's new sexual aggressiveness? B. Lyman Steward, a urologist at Cedars of Lebanon Hospital in Los Angeles, attributes the rising frequency of impotence among his male patients to the women's movement, which he calls an effort to dominate men. Perhaps a certain number of men who in the first place were uncertain of their sexuality have been intimidated by women's new aggressiveness, becoming so anxious that they are unable to perform. But a man who feels sure of himself sexually is unlikely to be impotent with a woman. He will avoid the woman who is unduly aggressive and hostile and welcome one who, heretofore shy about displaying her feelings, now feels freer in the sexual act. Sex can be either an exploitation, in which one partner uses the other out of hate, or it can be a sharing, out of love, with heightened sexual pleasure for both.

It is natural for a woman to want revenge for having been exploited as a little girl by her parents. And "the best revenge is living well," as the old adage puts it. But to live well requires self-esteem and confidence, which has not been easy to achieve for many women, brought up as they were to deny feelings of anger.

Chapter 6

THE DOLL-BABY

The little girl's fantasy that she wants her father to give her a baby, just as he impregnated her mother, has a deep impact on the lives of many women.

One fifty-year-old woman who had a hysterectomy was saying to her psychoanalyst, tears rolling down her cheeks, "More than anything in life I wanted a baby. Now it's too late. And I feel an unspeakable emptiness."

The psychoanalyst, knowing she had been married twice, asked, "Why didn't you have a child during your marriages?"

"I didn't do anything to stop from having a baby," she replied. "I just never got pregnant."

Then she added, "But I did get pregnant two other times. By men to whom I wasn't married. And I had abortions. I didn't think it fair to bring up the baby without a father."

"The man could have got a divorce and married you," said the psychoanalyst.

"I didn't want either of them to," she said. "I wouldn't let them, when they offered."

"It looks as though you unconsciously fixed it *not* to have a baby. One part of you may have wanted one, but a more powerful part did not."

During her analysis this woman became aware she had indeed "fixed" it so that when it was practical to have a baby, she could not conceive, but when it was impractical, she got pregnant—each time with a married man, like her father. Then she had to get rid of the babies because she felt so guilty at her unconscious wish to have her father's child, thereby displacing her mother in his affections. Her father was a man she had always adored and to whom she had never been able to break her erotic attachment, substituting a more appropriate male.

If a woman has never worked through her Oedipal feelings for her father, which means accepting them as natural childhood wishes and also accepting their inevitable frustration, she may never want another man's baby. Or she may go through a series of abortions. Or have an illegitimate child that she must then give up. Or, if married, she may be beset by crippling, bizarre fears during her pregnancies. In almost every woman there remains some residue of the fantasy that she will get rid of her mother and marry her father. To the extent this arouses guilt in adult life, the pregnant woman is likely to feel she will die because of her death wish for her mother.

For the unwed mother, it does not matter who the real father of her baby is, for in her unconscious it is always her own father. Her feelings about the baby, born out of forbidden desires, are apt to make the baby's life, as well as her own, emotionally difficult, even though illegitimacy is no longer such a stigma.

A woman may have an abortion for a number of conscious reasons such as lack of money to bring up the child or hatred of the man who impregnated her, but underlying them all is a sense of guilt because she has acted on the fantasy that she wants only her father's baby, which is taboo. Since she fears the punishment of death, the death of the fetus seems preferable to her own. Dreams that reveal this conflict occur with striking frequency in many a pregnant woman, according to psychoanalysts. The dreams also appear in the days immediately preceding menstruation when women who have had sexual intercourse without taking precautions fear they may be pregnant.

The bleeding of menstruation causes the emergence of many fantasies, according to Karen Horney. She wrote, "Every woman's analysis shows that with the appearance of menstrual blood, cruel impulses and fantasies of both an active and a passive nature are awakened in her." These are often preceded, in the days before menstruation actually begins, by feelings of self-depreciation, and depression—all of which recede, however, at the onset of the bleeding, when the woman feels relief.

Horney theorizes that tensions experienced during the premenstrual days "reveal we are dealing here with women who for some reason take frustrations poorly, who react to them with rage, but cannot deflect any or only some of this rage to the outside and who therefore turn it against themselves."

She does not mention what these "frustrations" might be. But possibly one reason for the relief felt by women when their blood starts to flow is that they now have proof they are not pregnant by their fathers.

Whether they have had recent sexual intercourse with a man does not matter, for the unconscious wish to become pregnant by the father is there. Thus, their conscious relief at the sight of the blood.

In women who do become pregnant, many fantasies, both conscious and unconscious, may cause them to feel undue terror at a time in their lives when they should be happiest. Some of these fantasies are founded on justifiable fears, but countless others are based on unreal fears.

In earlier days, when there was a high mortality rate at childbirth, it was realistic for a woman to fear death. Today this is no longer valid, yet many pregnant women still act as though they face death.

The opposite fantasy—that the baby will die in lieu of the mother—is equally common, even though the chances of that happening are also negligible today. The proportion of live births reported as attended by physicians of the leading hospitals in the United States is nearly 100 percent.

One woman said, "Why should I bother furnishing a room for the baby? I don't expect it to live. Either the doctor will injure it and kill it, or the baby will suffocate before it makes its way out of me."

The fantasy a baby will die is connected to the mother's fear of her own death and her wish that the baby die before it destroys her. One woman, who overate during her pregnancy, imagined the fetus as a tiny, devouring cannibal, bent on destroying her. Analysis brought out that this image of the cannibalistic fetus was rooted in her own infantile fantasies of wishing to devour her mother.

She recalled that when she was a little girl, her mother and father sometimes played "eating games" with her, nibbling her toes and hands, pretending to gobble her up and saying, "You're so adorable, I could eat you!" She felt frightened at first, then hid her fear with laughter.

She joined with other little girls as they played "eating games" to reassure themselves no one was really eaten, that it was all make-believe.

One day she became aware of her mother's protruding abdomen. Pointing to it, she asked, "What's that?"

"It's a new baby," said her mother.

"You must have loved it a lot," the little girl said.

"Why do you say that?" Her mother was puzzled.

"You ate it up."

Because her mother had told her that she loved her enough to "eat" her, the little girl imagined her mother had devoured the new baby.

For many women, pregnancy is a time when fantasies of loss, injury, and death may be activated, according to Helen E. Deutsch. She says, "The optimistic idea 'I shall have a child' assumes the character of an ecstatic experience that is at once opposed by the pessimistic negation 'I shall have no child, I have no right to have one, I shall lose it, I shall pay for it with my death.' "

Dr. Joseph Rheingold observes in his book, *The Fear of Being a Woman,* that he sometimes senses while witnessing the birth of a child "that the mother is destroying, not just delivering the baby." He notes that he has not known a pregnant woman in private practice, in the clinic, or in the hospital, who was entirely free of anxiety. His book offers a graphic picture of how negatively a mother can influence her daughter's pregnancy—a theme inherent in its subtitle, *A Theory of Maternal Destructiveness.*

Rheingold maintains that for many women pregnancy is the most intense threat to security and creates the greatest personal crisis in their lives because motherhood establishes equality with one's own mother and poses "the last and most menacing threat" for daring to achieve that equality. He believes most mothers unconsciously contest every step of the daughter's progress toward maternity and ". . . it would seem as if all the maternal maneuvers were directed by a single purpose: the daughter must not bear a child. Defiance of the mother is punishable by mutilation or death." Thus, bearing a child, he maintains, "more powerfully activates the death threat than any other event in a woman's life." She feels that to appease her mother she must destroy the child, but the child is also an object of her love, and so she is caught in a difficult dilemma, what Dr. Rheingold calls "trapped in a desperate conflict: kill the mother and preserve the baby or kill the baby and preserve the mother."

This conflict begins in pregnancy and may cause women to feel depressed as they fear "the menace of maternal vengeance." Rheingold makes it clear he does not think of maternal destructiveness as willful and culpable behavior, saying mothers are not consciously responsible, in that "the most virulent mother was once a hurt and frightened child," merely passing on from her own mother the feelings she experienced.

How a woman reacts to the idea of having a baby, says Dr. Hyman Spotnitz, mirrors the way her own mother reacted when she was born. He adds, "Fortunately, in spite of their fear of maternal vengeance, most women have such a strong wish to show up their mother and to prove they can be a far, far better mother than she, they decide to take on all risks and have the baby."

Aside from a pregnant woman's fears for her own or her baby's life, there is the fear she will give birth to a monster. This fantasy is probably as old as civilization itself, for it appears in drawings on the walls of the cavemen, in ancient Greek myths, and in the legends of every primitive society. A woman's first words after giving birth are usually "Is my baby normal?"

One woman, about to give birth, confessed to a

friend, "In spite of knowing the chances are nil, I'm afraid my child will be born deformed or mentally retarded."

"Why are you so afraid?" asked her friend.

"Everyone seems to want to frighten me, predicting the child may not be normal. Even my mother warned me that I must love the child no matter what it may look like. And I don't take drugs—not even aspirin!"

Why, with a very low percentage of deformities at birth, is this fear so universal? According to psychoanalysts, it reflects the woman's fantasy of *herself* as a monster, a mutilated being in a world of "perfect" men, a deformed creature who can give birth only to another one of its kind. This may be one reason so many women wish to have boys, for then they can identify with the "perfect" human being.

Too, women feel they may transmit to their unborn child their own "monstrous" wishes or nature. The popular book *Rosemary's Baby,* by Ira Levin, is based on several fantasies about pregnancy. For one, there is the fantasy, mentioned above, that the woman gives birth to a monster. For another, the fantasy that the act of sex which creates the baby is wicked and evil, the rape of an innocent woman by the "devil," man. And the fantasy that closes the book, that the mother, in spite of having given birth to a monster, will love it—the message that mother love will triumph even over monsterdom.

In some cases both husband and wife prefer to adopt a child rather than run the risk of producing a deformed baby. Hospitals are aware of this fear and almost the first thing a nurse does after delivery is to hold up the baby, showing the parents that all its parts are intact.

Women also commonly have the fantasy that if they do not produce a boy they have failed in motherhood. Indeed, some nations today allow a man to divorce a woman if she cannot bear him a son. Literature contains

descriptions of primitive rites in which little girls, unes-
teemed, were sacrificed to the gods.

Some pregnant women admit readily they want a
boy. According to one, "If I could not be a boy, at least I
want to create one." The late Dr. Flanders Dunbar told
of a woman who, upon being informed she had given
birth to a fine, healthy daughter, burst into tears and said
bitterly, "All that for a measly girl!" Another woman, who
grew up believing her mother and father wanted her to
be a boy, said, "Somehow I feel I owe my mother a son
because I failed her by turning out to be a girl."

Some women want a boy because they think a boy has
it easier in life. As one woman said, "I don't want a girl,
who will grow up and have to face the agonizing problems
I've had because I was a woman." Still others cannot bear
the thought of giving birth to a son, which reminds them
of their envy of men. Also, such women may be afraid of
the masculine part of themselves and fear coping with
what they see as problems surrounding the control of
strong aggressive and sexual drives in boys.

What to most women is an unspeakable fantasy has
probably occurred to every pregnant woman at one time
or another, whether she awaits her first or fifth child—
abortion. A fair percentage of spontaneous abortions,
those not deliberately induced, may have been brought
on because of the deep desire in the mother, either conscious or unconscious, to get rid of an unwanted child.
Many miscarriages frequently attributed to falls, frights,
and other accidents may also be, in large part, determined
by the underlying wish of the mother not to have the
baby, according to Dr. Spotnitz, author of *How To Be
Happy Though Pregnant.*

He says the unacceptable feeling, "I hate the baby
within," may be projected as "This baby inside hates me,
and therefore I will get rid of it before it does me in." If

a mother believes her baby will hate her when it emerges, she is usually afraid of her own hatred toward the child.

Sometimes, if a woman's childhood relationship with siblings was particularly intense, she will want to get rid of her baby as she wished her mother had done with her brothers and sisters, Spotnitz asserts. One of his patients had two abortions before she finally gave birth. During her analysis, she realized the abortions represented the unconscious killing of her two siblings.

"I couldn't understand why I was driven to get rid of two babies, and nót the third," she told Dr. Spotnitz. "One day I asked myself, 'Why *two*?' What magic was there in 'two'? Then I realized I had two competitors in life, my brother and sister." She allowed her own baby to be born only *after* she had unconsciously eliminated the rivals for her mother's love.

In the unconscious of every woman, according to Freud, a child represents both feces and a penis. The birth of a child restores to a mother, in fantasy, her lost feces and her lost penis, and if she has intense emotional conflicts she may cling to the child, preventing it from separating emotionally from her, because of this fantasy.

Declaring that the most evident connection is between "child" and "penis," Freud pointed out that both are called "the little one" (*das Kleine*) in German. He said the phrase, which originally meant the male genital organ, may have achieved a secondary application to the female genital, the clitoris.

Freud explained, "In some women, we not infrequently meet with the repressed wish to possess a penis. In other women, this wish is replaced by the wish for a child. It looks as if such women had understood (although this could not possibly have acted as a motive) that nature has given children to women as a substitute for the penis that has been denied them. From other women, again, we learn that both wishes co-existed in infancy, and that one had replaced the other. At first they wanted a penis like a man; then at a later, though still infantile stage there appeared instead the wish for a child."

A child, in the fantasy of a little girl in the anal stage, is regarded as feces, something which becomes detached from the body by passing through the bowel. A certain amount of what Freud called "libidinal cathexis [energy]" originally attached to the bowel is now extended to the child born through the bowel. "Linguistic evidence of this identity of child and feces is contained in the expression 'to *give* someone a child,' " Freud wrote. "For its feces are the infants's first gift, a part of his body which he will give up only on persuasion by a loved person, to whom, indeed, he will make a spontaneous gift of it as a token of affection, since as a rule infants do not soil strangers." He adds there are similar, if less intensive reactions, with urine.

The process of defecation presents the child with the first occasion upon which he must decide between a narcissistic or an object-loving attitude, according to Freud. He either parts obediently with his feces, "offering them up" to the mother he loves, or retains them for auto-erotic gratification and, later, as a means of angrily asserting his will. The latter act leads to defiance and obstinacy, "a quality which springs, therefore, from a narcissistic clinging to the pleasure of anal erotism," Freud explains.

The interest in feces is later carried on partly as an interest in money and partly as a wish for a child, thereby creating a fusion of anal-erotic and genital impulses, Freud concludes.

The emotionally healthy pregnant woman has comfortably assimilated all the pregenital fantasies, and if the relationship between her husband and herself is a secure one she will not have a terrifying time giving birth. She will welcome the thought of having a baby.

Helene Deutsch points out that if the expected child is "wished for, loved, expected with joy," pregnancy will be "a blessing." But if the child is "an involuntary burden, an object of future hatred in the mother's fantasy, of hatred still unopposed by conciliatory maternal feelings," pregnancy is "a curse." Thus we see here the importance for the psychosexual development of a little girl of her mother's fantasies and feelings about her in the very process of her birth.

Chapter 7

MIRROR, MIRROR ON THE WALL

A sixty-year-old widow, whose husband left her independently wealthy, spends almost the entire day making herself chic and beautiful. She passes hours at the beauty parlor, in the expensive boutiques of department stores. When she visits friends, she constantly inspects herself in a mirror to make sure she looks perfect. If a fingernail breaks, she has a temper tantrum, as though she had lost the finger, not merely a replaceable fragment of it.

A friend asked one day in exasperation, "How do you justify spending your entire life on beautifying your body?"

The woman did not get angry but said seriously, "What else is there to do? I live to please myself. I don't care what anyone else thinks as long as I know I look my very best each moment I am out in public."

This is an extreme example of how hundreds of thousands of women feel, judging by the advertising in newspapers, magazines, and on television. Commercial products promise a woman youth and beauty, no matter what her age. Women even resort to surgery to maintain the illusion of youth. It is not unusual for an actress or society leader to undergo several face-lifting operations as she ages.

The fantasy of eternal youth is common to every woman at one time or another. And yet, psychoanalysts tell us, a woman must learn to accept the natural process of growing old if she wants to overcome the fear of death —the culmination of old age. Only in the quiet acceptance of aging *as a part of life* will a woman achieve inner peace in her later years. Otherwise, she fights a losing battle against reality.

The woman who believes she must be eternally youthful is the woman also beset by the underlying feeling she has never really "lived," that ahead of her still lie exciting, romantic experiences. She exists in the world of adolescent illusion. She has not been able to accept maturity, preferring to dwell in a fairy tale world.

Several fantasies underlie a woman's obsessive wish to remain a beautiful "doll." She wishes to play the part of the little girl still dependent on her mother. She is also asking, "Mirror, mirror, on the wall, who is the fairest of them all?" This vain preoccupation, in part, reveals her girlhood wish to compete with her mother for her father. Psychologically she has never come to grips with the Oedipal conflict, accepted as natural the inevitable frustration of her wish to take her father from her mother.

One woman of forty-two, the mother of three children, admitted to her analyst, "When I look into a mirror, I see myself as an eighteen-year-old, getting ready to go out on a date." Such a woman is a perpetual adolescent.

She yearns for romantic fulfillment more than an intimate, lasting relationship with one man. She has remained in an earlier stage of psychosexual development, a less difficult one to cope with.

Women seem to live with romantic fantasies more than do men. Men are more apt to use sex as a way of discharging sexual tension—and society has accepted this as their right. Whereas women tend to attach illusions of romance to *every* sexual encounter. As little girls they were reading love stories while boys were out playing baseball and football to sublimate their sexual urges.

The narcissistic woman, whose main object in life is to stay young and look beautiful, appears infatuated with herself. If she marries, it is for money or social position or to feel less lonely. She craves the constant admiration of others. She seems self-centered, interested in people only if they are able to enhance her ego. She spends little or no time caring about what happens to others, even those close to her, unless it is a son or daughter—whom she regards merely as an appendage to herself, not as a person in his or her own right.

Narcissism wears many disguises. It may be hidden under the mask of a false solicitude about others. The femme fatale, who sets out to conquer men, basically loves only herself. According to Helene Deutsch, "The female Don Juan is . . . narcissistic; she cannot bear renunciation and negates it by changing her love objects—'I am loved in spite of everything.' " "Everything" means all her faults, including her inability to remain faithful to one man.

Deutsch points out that many women are often incapable of maintaining a harmonious relationship under "prosaic, humdrum conditions, because for them love is possible only as an ecstasy of admiration and of being constantly desired." She adds, "It is hard to satisfy this narcissistic need in the grind of everyday life." Such hunger in a woman finds appeasement only in a continuous stream of men who show desire for her.

Some narcissistic women adopt another kind of defense. They act out the fantasy of making one man happy in order to achieve the feeling, "This man is wonderful, and since I am part of him I am wonderful too." Eventually, however, they will hate the man, blaming him for their loss of identity. Slavish adoration inevitably contains buried hatred, which can be repressed only so long before it erupts—sometimes with disastrous consequences.

According to Deutsch, there exist what she calls two "fully conscious fantasies" in the normal girl relating to her father which show up in extreme form in the narcissistic woman. In the first fantasy, he is seen as a heroic man who deserves a better fate than marriage to her "prosaic" mother. She, the little daughter, would be a far more suitable object of his love, though she understands he must painfully renounce this choice. When an adult single woman remains tied all her life to a married (i.e., ineligible) man, she is caught in the fantasy of "painful love yearning" and in the suffering that is a repetition of her frustrated love for her childhood father. Such feelings, Deutsch says, "often prove stronger motives for faithfulness than the fulfillment of love."

The second "girlish fantasy" that often exerts a great influence on a woman's erotic life, Deutsch states, is based on the belief her father loves her mother as a sexual object, but gives "his better self, his ideal ego" to his daughter. She is the one who *really* understands him and "possesses his soul." Deutsch maintains that the woman who, after each sexual intimacy, anxiously asks the man if he still loves her, is not necessarily wishing to be reassured that by giving herself sexually to him she has not lowered herself in his esteem, but is really expressing the little girl's wish to share "the better things" with her lover as she did with her father. She wants to hear her lover say he loves her for her mind and "soul" as well as for her body.

The narcissistic woman looks on a man as the idolized father of her girlhood. When she spends all her time dressing up, wishing to be forever youthful, she is in fantasy the little girl trying to win Daddy's love. The mature woman accepts a man without overestimating him. This means she also accepts herself as an unidealized image, sees herself as a human being with faults and weaknesses, not needing to be a "perfect" being who will remain forever young and beautiful.

Narcissism is a denial of reality and death—the woman always peering at herself anxiously in the mirror is afraid to confront this truth. Some women go to the opposite extreme and kill themselves prematurely out of a narcissistic need. Successful Hollywood actresses have committed suicide when a famous actor has rejected them after a love affair. The narcissistic wound is so great, they cannot face their friends who, they believe, will look on them with great pity and contempt for being jilted. The rejection arouses memories of what they consider the tragic triangle in which they grew up, where they also played the part of the rejected one.

This triangle—mother, father, and daughter—is never completely forgotten by any woman, for it is the deepest emotional relationship she has during the most impressionable and vulnerable years of her life. It succeeds another relationship, an even older and more enduring one—the dual relationship between mother and daughter. According to Deutsch, it is not accurate to say the little girl "gives up her first mother relation in favor of the father." Rather she "gradually draws him into the alliance" with her mother, thereby creating the less exclusive triangular parent-daughter relationship.

As the daughter develops, she continues the "trio", just as she does the "duo" (though in a weaker and less elemental form), all through her life. The principal change is that the mother has been somewhat supplanted by the father. But the narcissistic woman is unable to give herself wholeheartedly, as she must for a while, to love of her father, wishing too intensely to remain attached emotionally to a mother who will take care of her.

During pregnancy, a woman prepares psychologically for the triangle of her childhood to be repeated with the birth of her baby. A narcissistic woman will say, "*I* want a child," relegating the man to the background. A mature woman will say, "*We* want a child."

All little girls (and boys) are by nature narcissistic, feeling omnipotent—as though the world revolved around them, with their mothers existing only to fulfill their every wish. But as a little girl grows, she is expected by her parents and society to become less selfish and to consider the feelings of others. If her parents set an example of thoughtfulness and generosity, she will feel self-esteem. But if parents, no matter how much they preach the opposite, are selfish and indulgent in their own lives, the little girl is apt to remain narcissistic.

Little girls may go to extremes in order to maintain some semblance of self-esteem in the face of a very destructive mother. This is shown in *Sybil*, written by Flora Rheta Schreiber. As a little girl Sybil had to split herself into many different personalities in an attempt to cope with the barbarism of her psychotic mother, who tortured her both physically and psychologically. Dr. Cornelia Wilbur, Sybil's therapist, commented on a recent television show that every case she knew in which a man or woman had several personalities involved their abuse as a child by a parent.

The woman who starves herself to look like a fashion model acts out of narcissism, as does the woman who overeats, who cannot deny herself food. All the will power in the world will not help the thin woman eat more in order to keep healthy, or the fat woman to eat less—for the same reason: they are unaware of being prisoners of their infantile fantasies. The compulsive eater always feels hungry and must satisfy that craving. To deprive her of food forces her to retreat into a deep depression or to feel intolerably angry. Compulsive eating gratifies in a symbolic way several unconscious desires. For one, the wish to feel loved. The woman who overeats gives herself the gift of food, a gift first bestowed by her mother.

Dr. Karl Abraham explains the connection between food and love: "The idea of a proof of love is inseparable from that of a *gift.* The first proof of love, which creates a lasting impression on the child and is repeated many times, is feeding from the mother." The overeater indulges her wish to be an infant fed by a mother who loves her and will refuse her nothing.

Abraham also says that erotic feelings occur in the taking in of food because it acts "as an agreeable stimulus to the child's erotogenic zones"—the mouth and anus. This erotic quality has also been noted by Dr. Therese Benedek, who comments that overeating leads in fantasy to "alimentary orgasm."

To the overeater, food brings a temporary sense of security and peace. As one woman said, "When I'm upset, I consume chocolate in any form—cake, candy, ice cream. Then, for the moment, I feel calm, as if nothing can touch me." The chocolate acts as a soporific, a "fix."

Another need filled by overeating is the symbolic release of anger. One woman writer said, "Often during the day, as I work, people phone just to pass the time in pleasant chatter. I feel angry but listen. After they've finished talking, I make a beeline for the fridge and devour everything in sight. I know it's because I'm furious at whoever has called, for interrupting my work. I chew food instead of chewing them out—or up."

Such compulsive eating gratifies the repressed wish to kill—to angrily destroy the enemy with one's teeth and mouth. The original unconscious implication of compulsive eating, Dr. Gustav Bychowski says, is the "securing of the mother in the most primitive form—introjection, which is cannibalistic incorporation of her." With each bite, unconsciously the woman who overeats is psychically devouring her mother of infancy, as an act of reassurance that she possesses her wholly, but also as vengeance at someone she once felt was a cruel mother who hated her and wished her dead. The bliss offered by the food is never "pure," states Bychowski, for guilt inevitably follows the aggressive wish to devour the mother. A woman's conscious guilt may be expressed as "I am getting fatter and fatter and I hate myself for it," but her unconscious guilt stems from her belief she is being punished for her cannibalistic impulses.

The mature woman enjoys food for its own sake, and she also wishes to live in harmony with the man she loves. The immature woman cannot make this differentiation: psychologically she wants to swallow her loved ones. Ideally, the little girl learns to distinguish two groups of objects she likes: food, which she may swallow, and parents (later other human beings, animals, toys, etc.), which she must not swallow or put into her mouth. She learns to substitute for the acts of biting and swallowing acts that do not destroy the loved one—kissing and caressing. "Wooing is substitute for raping," in the words of Dr. Ludwig Eidelberg.

Thus cannibalism—the destructively aggressive part of the little girl's first relationship with her mother—is given up in fact, though not in fantasy, as she relinquishes her mother as food and accepts instead the food her mother prepares for her. She inhibits her hostile wish to devour her mother, turning it against herself when she gets angry (unhappy people eat themselves up, in a sense). The little girl now wishes to see, to smell, to hear, and to touch her mother.

Acceptance of her mother's prohibition against biting and eating her is based on the little girl's identification with her mother. Most of our cannibalistic urges are suppressed to such a degree we would rather starve than eat another human being. In rare cases we hear of a psychotic adult who eats human flesh, or survivors of an airplane crash who have done so to keep alive. This is a return to the earliest of impulses, supposedly repressed beyond all acting out.

The use of sarcasm, the "biting word," reveals in symbolic fashion the repressed wish to destroy an enemy with the mouth. The sarcastic woman indulges in verbal cannibalism as she masks an intense fury from infant days. A vitriolic woman undoubtedly is raging at a mother she feels did not care for her tenderly enough.

A little girl has fantasies that eating will produce a baby, having seen her mother's abdomen bulge when she became pregnant, and the little girl's wish for her father's baby may be expressed in overeating. This was graphically pictured by Robert Lindner in his account of Laura in *The Fifty-Minute Hour.* He describes the oral orgies of this young woman suffering from bulimia, a pathological craving for food. Lindner states he had never heard of anyone with so intense a need for overeating. During episodes of extreme depression, Laura became ravenous, insatiable. "Until she reached a stage of utter exhaustion, until her muscles no longer responded, until her distended insides protested with violent pain, until her strained senses succumbed to total intoxication, she would cram herself with every available kind of food and drink," Lindner reported.

Laura told him: "One minute I'm fine, feeling gay, busy, loving life and people. The next minute I'm on an express highway to hell . . . I think it begins with a feeling of emptiness inside. Something, I don't know what to call it, starts to ache; something right in the center of me feels as if it's opening up, spreading apart maybe. It's like a hole in my vitals appears. Then the emptiness starts to throb . . . Soon I feel as if there's nothing to me but a vast, yawning space surrounded by skin that grabs convulsively at nothingness . . . The sensation changes from an ache to a hurt, a pounding hurt. The feeling of emptiness becomes agony."

She would gorge herself until she was unconscious, until her abdomen became swollen and she retched, her body refusing to take in any more food. She would then sleep for two days and nights, during which she had "sick dreams" she could hardly recall. On waking, she felt completely disgusted with herself.

Lindner saw Laura four times a week for two years, as she talked of a childhood in which her mother, a cripple in a wheelchair, fought constantly with a husband who usually came home drunk. Laura's mother would refuse to serve him supper, and accuse him of spending his money on other women. One night he walked out on his family for good. Laura had openly adored her father, hated her mother. During analysis, she became aware that her eating binges masked, for one thing, her unconscious wish to have a baby by her father. She also realized how deeply her life had been affected by the violent behavior of her parents and how she sought solace in overeating, a narcissistic defense her mother had also used to combat anxiety.

Another analytic patient, each time her session ended, would head for the nearest ice cream parlor and order a hot fudge sundae to fill an overwhelming craving. She was thirty pounds overweight and unable to diet. Analysis revealed each time she left the analyst's office she felt rejected, as though he had thrown her out after loving her for fifty minutes. To make up for this feeling of hurt inflicted by a man to whom, in the transference process, she attached the same feelings of love and hate she felt for a father who had left home when she was ten, she sought solace in a childhood dessert. The chocolate fudge represented her once-cherished feces—which, in the little girl's anal fantasy, represented a "loving gift" to her mother. On the even earlier oral level, the ice cream represented the sweetness and substance of her mother's first gift—milk. On the later genital level, as in the case of Laura, the overeating symbolized the wish to be pregnant—the fantasy that if she ate enough, her stomach would grow big with her father's child.

Compulsive or narcissistic eating may also occur out of anxiety over separation. It is no coincidence we overeat when we leave home to go on trips; we stuff ourselves with food to make up for the pangs of separation from the familiar.

Overeating also symbolically fulfills a woman's wish to devour the rivals of infancy—the other children her mother had or anyone who later represents them in her mind.

One woman in analysis noted that after a telephone call from either her sister or brother she would become very hungry. She told her analyst, "I am driven to devour food as I feel they devour me—my time—when they spend hours telling me about their petty problems."

"And what about your wish to devour them?" the analyst asked.

"You must admit it's safer eating food than people," she quipped.

"It's even safer if you can assert yourself and ask them not to call you when you are busy," he replied.

At the opposite extreme, the woman who starves herself, who looks like a concentration camp victim, is strenuously denying her early cannibalistic, destructive wishes. She is afraid to express her hostile desire to devour, consuming just enough to stay alive. One such woman admitted, "I fear if I ever let go I would eat everything in sight." Anorexia conceals a deep rage at the feeding mother.

All of us, in moments of stress, wish to return to the comforting, sensual pleasures of infancy, when there were few frustrations,—a time, in Freud's words, of "primary love." In such a tension-free love, as Dr. Michael Balint points out, there is no need for the infant to test reality, no need for what he calls "any work of conquest." If, however, a mother is not in harmony with the child's desires and proves too frustrating during these early months of life, severe emotional damage may occur as a result of the mother's narcissistic tendencies.

Next to food, alcohol is possibly the second greatest narcissistic addiction for women. Many use it in moderate degree to reduce fear and feel freer sexually. The alcohol warms the blood, removes inhibitions. Alcohol helps to release narcissistic feelings: a woman too shy to admire herself when she is sober, after a few drinks, may look in a mirror and say to herself, "I'm really very attractive, why don't I do something about it?" She may then go to a bar, pick up a stranger, and have sex. Rarely, however, does this lead to a permanent alliance.

"I'd never have sex if I didn't get slightly drunk," a thirty-year-old woman confessed to her analyst.

He pointed out that the use of alcohol to dull the senses so sexual fear may be denied is more destructive than the use of food. Overeating may cause physical illnesses in the long run, but alcohol intensifies destructive wishes immediately. Violent impulses often emerge, overwhelming feelings of tenderness and caring. Many an angry word is spewed out that tears apart a relationship. Some women may commit murder when they are drunk, later resorting to the excuse, "I don't remember a thing," as a way of denying responsibility for their acts. It may be true they have blacked out, but their unconscious thought processes were functioning as they acted out hidden wishes. If proof were needed of the existence of the unconscious, it is furnished in the actions of alcoholics after they have lost consciousness, leaving underlying primitive thinking to dominate.

The symbolism of alcohol seems clear: the bottle represents the breast and the liquid symbolizes the mother's milk and its warming effect on the body, giving a false sense of security and comfort. Women who become drug addicts may be even more deeply depressed than alcoholics. The addict clings to her drugs with the same despair shown by the depressed woman clinging to her image of the lost loved one, says Abraham.

One particular fantasy of drug addicts, to merge with the mother, is more evident than in food or alcohol addiction, psychoanalysts maintain. The ingestion of drugs via syringe and needle symbolizes the umbilical cord tying mother and fetus. The drug addict would appear to be the most regressed addict.

Many women take drugs on a milder scale—sleeping pills at night or benzedrine in the morning—to feel less depressed. One woman said to her analyst, "I couldn't get through the day without an upper before lunch, or a downer at night."

"Perhaps you will be able, after a while, to face the feelings that are causing you such anxiety, and lose your need for drugs," he said.

It took two years before she was able to be aware of those feelings, understand her conflicts, and no longer need drugs, either day or night. She was able at last to face her psychic pain.

Sex is a popular addiction these days, given women's new sexual freedom. Sex becomes an addiction when it does not arise out of the sharing of love, but to fulfill a narcissistic need. The sex addict considers sex not a pleasure to be enjoyed, but an obsession, something she *must* have in order to live. After each orgasm, she feels "good," reassured and confident for the moment. But immediately she must race to another man, and another, and another. To such a woman sex is more important than anything in life—work, friends, social activities. Thoughts of sex take up most of her waking hours and her dreams.

One twenty-nine-year-old woman said to a friend, "I need an orgasm every night. I don't care if it's by the same man for a few weeks or months, or a different man each night. Otherwise, I feel like killing myself, I get so depressed." Not only is this woman unable to enjoy other satisfactions in life, but she does not truly enjoy sex. She admitted to her friend she never felt joy with a man, no matter how many orgasms she had, adding, "I always get out of bed feeling sad, wanting to cry."

Such a woman is compulsively seeking release from sexual tension, as though going to the bathroom for release of pressure on bladder or bowels. She does not *choose* a man, she is a victim of her unconscious fantasies. No one man will ever satisfy her, for she demands what no mortal man could give her—a feeling of confidence as a woman, a feeling that can only come from within.

Compulsive sex, like any other addiction, is used to

cover the feelings a woman does not wish to face. It is easier to escape into the addiction than to take on what seems the difficult task of finding out why she must resort to a life of promiscuity. She believes sex will solve all her problems, that if only she had enough sex, she would be able to bear her existence.

One fantasy underlying sex addiction, psychoanalysts say, is that each time she has intercourse she is symbolically taking away the man's penis. While consciously believing she is more feminine for engaging in many sexual affairs, convincing herself she is desired, unconsciously she feels triumphant—and then guilty—because, for the moment, she has deprived the man of the penis she both fears and covets (the castrating aspect of her action).

Sex addiction does not always imply promiscuity—that is, different partners. One wife insisted her husband have sex with her every night whether he felt like it or not. He complied for fifteen years, then rebelled. She was so upset and angry that she went to a psychoanalyst. During her analysis, she realized she had been driven by a compulsion that was unfair to her husband. She was narcissistically demanding nightly proof of his love. In a sense she was also demanding that he give his penis to her every night so she could feel the dominant one—the man.

A feeling of abusing both herself and her partner occurs if a woman uses sex for exploitation, if her need for sex is desperate. Sexual impulses do *not* always have to be gratified, says Dr. Milton R. Sapirstein: "The concept that people must be gratified every time they have a sexual impulse results disastrously, leaving the individual with very little toleration to frustration."

Sex should be a part of life, not the whole of it. Sex is not a matter of life and death, though the sex addict cannot accept this. To go without sex for very long to her feels like dying. Some women, if they cannot reach a climax, feel murderous toward the man, as though he has deprived them of the right to live.

Gambling is another popular addiction. Today, with more leisure time, larger earnings, and off-track betting, an increasing number of women are becoming gamblers. The woman gambler has regressed to an early period of infancy in which her fantasies are magically fulfilled. She believes, against all the known odds, that she will win. She is also indulging in an act of hostility against parents who forced her into the awareness that she was not omnipotent. Because of her guilt at such aggression, she has the unconscious desire to lose and be rejected by the outer world, according to Dr. Edmund Bergler.

He describes the gambler as "a naughty child who expects to be punished for his forbidden and aggressive acts. Basically, the *pleasant* component of the tension felt by the gambler is derived from the pleasure of aggressively used childish megalomania. The *painful* component arises from expectation of punishment for the 'crime.'"

Consciously, the woman who gambles is "absolutely convinced" she will win, Bergler says, but unconsciously she is convinced "the cruel mother or father will be exposed as a refuser," and make her lose. The "adversary" (the poker partner, the roulette wheel, the race track, the stock exchange) is always unconsciously identified with the refusing mother and father, Bergler maintains. He adds, "Only one thing can be expected from this 'monster' —refusal, denial and defeat. The gambler's unconscious wish to lose assures this defeat."

Why does one narcissistic woman choose as her addiction food, another drugs, a third alcohol? Our culture offers a number of outlets for addiction. In one group it may be fashionable to smoke, in another to drink, in a third to take drugs. As one social worker observed, "Years ago, it was the scene in black ghettos to use drugs. The whites are just catching up."

Many women do not need an addiction, so the question must be asked why a particular woman finds herself unable to endure life without becoming an addict, and why she chooses her special addiction. Only an intensive study of each woman's psychological life will furnish the reasons for her specific addiction. Perhaps she is imitating a mother or father, for an addiction is given sanction if a parent indulges in it, no matter how strongly the child is forbidden to follow suit. Sometimes a parent will even encourage an addiction, as when an overweight mother stuffs her little daughter at each meal and between meals, using food almost as a narcotic.

Eventually a woman will be destroyed by her addiction, for—as Freud warned—any excess carries within it the seeds of its own destruction.

As with many defenses, addictions stem in part from narcissism. Feeling unloved by her mother and father, the little girl has only self-love for reassurance. As a grown woman, she seeks to express that self-love in somewhat socially acceptable ways. The expansion after therapy of a woman's capacity to give love, with less need for self-love, is reported by psychoanalysts.

Dr. Heinz Kohut notes that a personal psychoanalysis results in both "nonspecific" and "specific" beneficial changes. The most prominent "nonspecific change," he says, is "the increase and the expansion of the patient's capacity for object love [love of another person]." He adds that the specific changes take place in the realm of narcissism itself as the narcissistic component of the total love experience becomes a subsidiary one. It is not that there is a "change of the mobilized narcissism into object love," he states, but that there is "a freeing of formerly repressed object libido." He amplifies: "There is a deepening and a refinement of the patient's love experience, whether in the state of being in love, in his long-term fondness of another human being, or in his devotion to cherished tasks and purposes."

The increased capacity to love another person is also due to a sharper sense of self-identity, Kohut believes: "The more secure a person is regarding his own acceptability, the more certain his sense of who he is, and the more safely internalized his system of values—the more self-confidently and effectively will he be able to offer his love without undue fear of rejection and humiliation."

Kohut also points out that what psychoanalysts call "the infantile grandiosity," the feeling that the world revolves around him, which every child experiences, becomes gradually built into the ambitions and purposes of the personality "and lends not only vigor to a person's mature strivings, but also a sustaining positive feeling of the right to success."

What Kohut describes as "the narcissistic mother" appears able to maintain a relationship with only one child at a time. Her "emotional restriction" can frequently be seen in the childhood history of patients suffering from narcissistic personality disorders whose emerging memories appear at first to point to the birth of a sibling as the primary cause of their disturbance, he explains. Then he states:

"It is, however, not the birth of a sibling which is to blame—most children do indeed survive this event without disabling fixations in the narcissistic realm—but the complete and sudden shift from the mother's narcissistic involvement with the new baby. To be exact, such mothers seem to be able to feel genuine emotions only for a small, preoedipal boy (the father is usually depreciated, and older children are usually dropped emotionally or ambivalently infantilized by her); but this relationship, while it lasts, is indeed a very intense one ... As soon as another child is on the way, however, the mother invests the new baby with the narcissistic cathexes which she withdraws from the older child with traumatic abruptness."

The woman whose childhood narcissism accompanies her into adulthood shows disturbances in her relationship to the "idealized" mother of infancy, Kohut declares. These disturbances he classifies into three groups, according to the developmental phase during which the main impact of the "trauma" with her mother was experienced:

1.   Very early disturbances in the relationship with the mother appear to lead to a general "structural weakness—perhaps a defective or malfunctioning stimulus barrier—that interferes broadly with the capacity of the psyche to maintain the basic narcissistic homeostasis [balance] of the personality." Someone thus afflicted suffers from "a diffuse narcissistic vulnerability."

2.   Later, but still during the preoedipal period, traumatic disturbances in the relationship with the mother, especially a traumatic disappointment in her, may interfere with the establishment of "the drive-controlling, drive-channeling, and drive-neutralizing basic fabric of the psychic apparatus." Internal and external conflicts, often shown in the form of perverse fantasies, may occur as a result of this defect.

3.   If the origin of the disturbance relates to the oedipal period, which starts about four or five years of age, or even as late as the beginning of the school years, the person "will forever search for external ideal figures from whom he wants to obtain the approval and the leadership which his insufficiently idealized superego cannot provide."

The narcissistic personality feels not so much guilt as shame, Kohut states. He reacts with excruciating embarrassment if he makes a *faux pas,* a slip of the tongue, is inappropriately dressed for a social occasion, or tells a joke at which nobody laughs.

"When examined in detail, the painfulness of many of these situations can be understood by recognizing that a rejection occurred, suddenly and unexpectedly, just at the moment when the patient was most vulnerable to it, i.e., at the very moment when he had expected to shine and was anticipating acclaim in his fantasies," he says.

The mental pain occurs partly because the person feels he is not in control in the very realm in which we all believe ourselves undisputed master—our own psyche, Kohut explains. The person's mind "returns again and again to the painful moment, in the attempt to eradicate the reality of the incident by magical means, i.e., to undo it." Simultaneously, he may "angrily wish to do away with himself in order to wipe out the tormenting memory in this fashion."

The torment felt by the narcissistic person can be seen during his personal psychoanalysis, Kohut notes, as he reveals his suffering, his painful embarrassment, and his anger that the act he has committed cannot be undone. Kohut warns that "childhood grandiosity and exhibitionism," which are part of the narcissistic personality, "must not be condemned," in that they arise out of childhood fears and hurts at the hands of narcissistic parents.

One woman in analysis at first resented it when the analyst firmly but gently kept pointing out to her how her need to feel "special" interfered with her feelings of self-esteem.

"I *don't* want to be special to anyone," she stormed. "My whole life has been devoted to helping others. I always put myself last."

"Because you really would like to be first," he said.

"That's ridiculous!" she snapped.

Then she started to be able to look at herself more clearly and to realize her hidden wish to be "first" in her mother's eyes. She was the youngest of three children and had always felt the two oldest came first, as they literally did, in her mother's affections.

One day she said to the analyst, "You were right when you said I wanted to be 'Numero Uno.' It took me a long time to realize this."

"Every child wants to be the first and only child," he said. "It is a blow to our self-esteem to realize we have to share our mother's love. No child gives up easily the illusion he is the only one."

"It's difficult to be a child." She sighed.

"It's more difficult to be an adult who still wishes to be a child," he commented.

The well-analyzed woman finds an increase in her feelings of empathy, creativity, humor, and thoughtfulness, psychoanalysts report. These characteristics were formerly blocked by her narcissism as she concentrated on herself to the virtual exclusion of the needs of anyone else. She now feels less "fragmented," able to achieve what Kohut calls "a greater cohesiveness of the self." This includes, he adds, "a sustaining positive feeling of the right to success."

The narcissism of early childhood, despite its central importance, is compelled to give way by two forces: first, by the child's dependency and thus the indispensability and value placed upon another person, and second, by the increasing awareness of his fantasies, wishes, and the sense of omnipotence that reality "contradicts, frustrates and denies," according to Dr. Gregory Rochlin.

He describes narcissism as "a stable lifesaving process which holds the seeds of discontent as well as those of restitution." Narcissism is part of the process of self-preservation and when that is threatened, narcissism protects it, he explains. Narcissism is indispensable to offset the dangers to self-esteem, "a complex process held in precarious balance that relies in great measure on narcissism to right it."

The excesses to which narcissism may be developed are always related to the "fragility of self-esteem," he says. He adds, "Moreover, careful study of narcissism has shown that the restoration of a lowered or lost self-esteem requires, in addition to vanity, an object relationship for libidinal gratification even if it must be gained in a pathological fashion."

He defines narcissism as "the libidinal component of the instinct of self-preservation," and self-esteem as "its ego manifestation." He states: "The executant functions of the ego, by skill, mastery, achievement, by controlling and manipulating and thus affecting the environment so as to provide a better adaptation to reality, sustain self-esteem. Conversely, when the executant functions do not develop sufficiently to make such aims possible, self-esteem suffers and a sense of one's precarious position or failure prevails."

In other words, narcissism does not turn into self-esteem, a conscious feeling, but accompanies it as the unconscious component. Both are affected by how much a woman accepts the world outside herself.

Rochlin makes the extremely important point that "animism," perceiving the world as having the qualities and characteristics of oneself, and as being governed by the eye-for-an-eye principle, and looking upon the world as a place where deeds can be undone and punished and in which magical thinking and magical happenings occur, "is part of every child's existence." He points out: "Despite increasing adaptation to reality and a sharper perception of it that contradicts childhood causality, childish beliefs are not altogether replaced; instead, the adult beliefs are added to them. The two coexist."

We never "give up" or "forget" our childish thinking but, as Rochlin says, "add" to it. The more of reality we are able to accept, the less our childish thinking will influence our acts.

The woman who lives as a doll, pursuing the illusion of eternal youth, may think she avoids the pain of growing old and dying. But in refusing to accept the reality of aging and of death, she dooms herself to a robot-like existence.

Chapter 8

"WOE IS ME"

There are women, young and old, who live in a morass of self-pity, fantasying themselves as martyrs on the stage of life. The martyr's behavior is designed to win pity, and often succeeds in that aim. But pity contains an underlying feeling of contempt. The woman who uses her martyrdom to inspire pity eventually finds herself scorned and deserted, for the burdens imposed by self-victimization are difficult for others to bear.

One woman said of a friend she reluctantly gave up, "All she talked about was the miserable blows life dealt her. Her conversation was one long complaint—how depressed she felt, her latest physical ache, and how no one really loved her in spite of all she did for so many people."

Another woman, who listened for years to a friend describe how she suffered at the hands of a tyrannical husband, said to her one day, her patience coming to an end, "Please take your complaints to a psychiatrist. I've had enough. My idea of a friend is someone who shares thoughts that are stimulating and pleasurable. Not one who uses me in place of a therapist."

Many husbands live years with a martyred wife, unconsciously needing the wife's suffering so they can express their own sadistic feelings. For martyrs are masochists who unconsciously enjoy suffering and who believe the suffering will bring them love. Masochism holds in it the suffering of the little girl who adores her father but is doomed to a love which must remain unrequited.

Martyrdom conceals hostility beneath a mask of super-compliance, and it is this hidden hostility others feel and bristle at. The woman who appears a martyr to her husband or children is saying, "I'll slave my life away to make you happy, sacrificing all my own wishes just to get your love." But this is a form of emotional blackmail. Such a woman is giving not out of love but to get love on demand. There is a great difference between true caring and martyring oneself out of a sense of guilt because of underlying angry feelings.

"See what I've done for you—how much of my life I've given up to make you happy," a woman tells a man, hoping in return he says, "I will love you forever because of your great selfless love for me." Instead, the man usually senses he is being bribed, threatened, and is apt to withdraw all feelings of love. Intimidation, conscious or unconscious, never calls forth genuine love. The martyr is doomed from the start: she does not offer a warm, permissive love, but a love that essentially seeks to control.

This wish to control, at the most primitive level, is the wish to castrate. The controlling, martyr-like woman is a castrating woman. Dr. Karen Horney explains that fear of the controlling, castrating woman "is an anxiety of psychogenic origin that goes back to feelings of guilt and old childhood fears. Its anatomical-psychological nucleus lies in the fact that during intercourse the male has to entrust his genitals to the female body, that he presents her with his semen and interprets this as a surrender of vital strength to the woman, similar to his experiencing the subsiding of erection after intercourse as evidence of having been weakened by the woman."

The martyred, controlling mother makes it difficult for her children to separate from her, to achieve their own identity. Like a dictator, she takes it upon herself to decide what is best for others. If her children eventually acquire enough emotional strength, they rebel and seek a life of their own. If they lack such strength, they remain emotionally crippled for life, rotting in their own repressed anger, so to speak.

Martyred women are depressed women. Their wish to be pitied, their excessive need for love, comes out of the early childhood feeling they were not loved, that their life was bleak and tormented—as no doubt it was, psychologically speaking. They have a right to feel depressed, though they are far from lovable as they inflict this depression on others in the form of martyrdom.

If a woman feels martyred, fantasies underlie her depression. One woman in analysis, who was becoming aware of how much of a martyr's role she had assumed in her marriage, had mourned her father's death for ten years. She eventually became able to acknowledge a deep hatred for him, a feeling she had always denied, conscious only of her adoration. She hated him in part because he was cruel to her mother, abandoning her to marry another woman. She also hated him because he struck her at times when, as a child, she dared disagree with him. As she grew up, this woman hid from herself all fantasies of revenge on the male, playing the martyr role as she had seen her depressed mother do.

Depression, when it is severe, brings with it the feeling of being unloved, unlovable, and incapable of loving. In its extreme form, depression is the feeling of utter helplessness in the face of overwhelming, terrifying emotions. This burden of psychic pain, in Freud's words, appears to "empty the ego," for depression lowers self-esteem. It may have harmful effects on both mind and body, ranging from partial disablement through physical illness to suicide.

What fantasies lie behind depression? The depressed woman, though usually not aware of it, is caught in the grip of a single powerful fantasy. The feeling of depression masks a childhood wish she considers dangerous to admit—the desire to kill the one who has hurt her. She has turned the wish, with its hatred and consequent guilt, inward. The result is deep suffering.

The degree of hatred is related to the degree of identification the child has formed with the "bad" mother. A little girl who has a controlling, hostile mother, will identify in part with her to try to get her love—"If I'm like you, then you won't hate me." By becoming like her mother she reassures herself nothing disastrous will happen to her. This is what Freud called "identification with the aggressor" in an attempt to survive psychically.

Sometimes a little girl may have difficulty in distinguishing between herself and her loved-hated mother. Hating her mother and hating herself become one and the same feeling.

When a depressed woman, for instance, hates a man who abandons her, with whom she feels merged, if she commits suicide, she is, in her fantasy, also killing him. This is how Freud explained what he called "the enigma of suicide." The woman may leave a note saying she hopes

the man suffers for what he has done to her but, unconsciously, she believes she is murdering him even as she
takes her own life. Rather than killing the man who re-
jects her, she loves him enough so she prefers to destroy
herself. The woman who kills the man who has abandoned her feels predominantly hate for him. She is less
depressed than the woman who commits suicide. The
main purpose of depression is to handle hostility in a
regressive way by turning the anger back on the self when
there is still a certain amount of love for the one who has
inflicted the hurt.

It may seem paradoxical that the act of suicide symbolizes murder. But, as Freud explained, the loved one in
fantasy has become a permanent part of the self-image. A
little girl whose mother leaves her alone a good deal of the
time, causing the child to become frightened, angry, and
then guilty because of her anger, reassures herself in fantasy that she possesses her mother inside her. She has, as
psychoanalysts say, orally incorporated her mother. To a
baby girl, "to know" is to possess, to put whatever she sees
—be it a person's thumb, a piece of dirt, or a cigarette butt
—into her mouth.

When a severe depression does not end in suicide or
murder, a woman will—because of her fantasy that the
wish is the same as the deed—punish herself for the guilt
she feels at the wish to murder someone who has hurt her.
She turns inward her murderous wishes, which are not
intense enough to drive her to murder or suicide. In a
sense, depression is a slow death of the self, administered
in small psychic doses for daring to wish a loved one dead.

The frequent physical illnesses of the martyred
woman show her need to punish herself, at the same time
that she asks to be pitied. Illness carries the demand, "I
am sick and helpless and you must take care of me, love
me." The martyred woman is living out a depression aris-

ing in infancy. When a woman is very depressed, the cause lies in her relationship to her mother and father, primarily her mother. The little girl cannot help but feel destructive wishes toward the mother who frustrates her, as every mother is bound to do to a certain extent. But she also wishes to save her mother from destruction, since if her mother dies, she will have no one to feed and love her. So she learns to turn her rage on herself. Guilt and depression are the results.

Psychoanalysts agree that the more disturbed, angry, and depressed the mother, the more disturbed, angry, and depressed the little girl. They also say the first months of life are the most important. It is then we experience all the traumatic "firsts"—the first sharp stab of jealousy, the first spurt of hatred when we cannot have what we want, the first hurt when we feel unloved, the first sense of fascination and fear about the sexual sensations of our bodies. It is also the time of greatest vulnerability, for we have not as yet learned how to use reason.

In these earliest months a mother's attitudes are conveyed to the little girl through everything she does— nursing, dressing, holding, bathing, diapering, even tucking her in and changing the sheets on her bed. The way a mother handles her, whether out of love or duty, or in fear and irritation, how she teaches her to talk, to walk, and to play—all these provide the emotional climate in which the little girl develops.

If a little girl is frightened of her mother, she will be frightened of her father and everyone else in life. She will also be frightened of her fantasies of revenge. Aggression that does not contain hostility is a normal feeling in the early months of life. It cannot be considered hostile unless there is too much frustration by the mother, until the little girl feels that through her negligent behavior the mother is expressing hatred toward her. The mother is the little girl's protector against her own helplessness and all outer dangers. However, if the mother herself proves to be the danger, the little girl lives in terror of her life. She is caught in an excruciating conflict: her fear of losing her mother versus her fear and hatred of her mother. To have her mother near is what matters most. Her mother's absence—both physical and emotional—is the greatest of all dangers, causing intolerable hurt, grief, hatred, then guilt, and finally depression.

Thus the rage inherent in a deep depression goes back to early fantasies of helplessness in the face of enormous threats, to a time the mother abdicated her role as protector. When something in a woman's current life depresses her, it has stirred memories of earlier hurts, earlier rages. A cutting remark by a friend, wounding a woman's self-esteem, may give rise to a depression replete with destructive fantasies from the oral, anal, and phallic stages of her life.

Every little girl has to give up, to some degree, the belief that she is one with her mother, that together they are all-powerful. She must learn to tolerate becoming separate in order to establish her own identity. If she does not relinquish the fantasy of symbiotic unity with her mother, she will face depression as an adult.

During the crucial time in a little girl's life when she first starts to separate, the mother, if she is adequately loving, "functions as a protective shield," in the words of Dr. Margaret Mahler. The mother takes care of the little girl in the first literal steps of separation, as she totters around a room. The mother makes sure the little girl does not hurt herself physically, rescuing her from bumping into sharp objects, or any situation that will produce anxiety and fear. Ideally, there exists what Mahler calls "a mutual cueing of mother and child." The little girl conveys to her mother her fears, and the mother conveys to her daughter the sense that she has understood and will protect her. If the mother misses her cues, if she does not protect her daughter, the little girl will feel her mother does not care about her. She will be hurt and angry, turn her anger and then her guilt inward, and become depressed.

Mahler reports that little girls who show "the basic depressive mood" do not possess much confidence or self-esteem. Too large a portion of their natural aggressive drive, which should be used for healthy growth, is diverted into defenses that ward off both their rage and their fear of annihilating the mother, as a result of their destructive fantasies. At the same time, such children struggle to restore the state of oneness with the mother, a state from which they should be emerging.

It is Mahler's theory that if motoric growth—sitting up, crawling, walking—occurs while there is still a lag in the child's emotional readiness to function separately from the mother, an "organismic panic" ensues. The psychic content of this "panic" is not readily evident because the child is still unable to communicate. It uses fantasies as a way of combatting the panic. A little girl's bodily growth continues, but her healthy emotional development has been hindered or thwarted, perhaps to such an extent that, unable to move out of her fantasy world, she may become psychotic. Psychosis is evidence that the loss of trust in the mother has been profound.

Mahler believes the early conflicts occurring in connection with this loss of trust are compounded by later difficulties—accepting a rival brother or sister, toilet training, castration anxiety, for example. She maintains that these later conflicts, while significant, are not the original conflicts. They do not in themselves generate the depressive mood, but "only accentuate, dramatize and compound the basically negative mood predisposition of the child."

She reports that the depressive response, with or without a generally angry mood, was observed in little girls "definitely more" than in boys. Mahler attributes this to "their anger about and disappointment with mother having not given them the penis," adding this "could be convincingly traced in several cases."

A little girl who is unable to develop successfully in a psychic sense during the first years of life because of poor emotional nurturing from her mother may erect such strong defenses against her hostile fantasies that a self-destructive pattern is established which persists throughout her lifetime. For instance, a woman may be obsessed by the "beachcomber" fantasy, the wish to escape from responsibilities, spend her days strolling along a beach, basking in the warmth of the sun, taking a dip in the ocean whenever she pleases, eating when she gets hungry, avoiding all pressures. Her idea of paradise is a return to the place and comfort of infancy, when she and her mother were alone in the world. Though we all have this wish to some degree (we take vacations precisely to get away from the pressure of work), it is only the very infantile person who succumbs completely to such a fantasy.

The death or desertion of a parent is felt by the child as a devastating blow to self-esteem, causing hostile fantasies of a destructive nature. When a little girl loses one parent, she will glorify that parent and divert her anger onto the other parent, Dr. Edith Jacobson points out. It is not unusual to hear a little girl blame her mother for having caused her father to leave home, no matter what the facts. According to Jacobson, the little girl has raised her lost father's "narcissistic value and meaning to the point of turning it into the most precious part of the self which has been lost and must be recovered." This explains, she says, why both little girls and boys refuse to accept, and struggle against, identifying with the remaining (to them, castrated) parent—the one left behind or abandoned, as the child feels it has been.

A martyred woman in her depression is in fantasy emulating her depressed mother. The child, as Anna Freud put it, "follows her [mother] into the depressive mood." She asserted this process was not merely identification with and imitation of the mother, but a response to the emotional climate which infected the child's psyche as a germ would the body.

One little girl believed her mother loved her only when she was depressed. When she was active, the mother, a very depressed woman, could not manage her, screamed at her, and threatened to leave her. So the daughter, to gain her mother's love, unconsciously sank into depression much of the time.

Day after day a woman may suffer small depressions caused by feeling rejected. She may want to strike back, but most of the time she does not, for she has been taught to repress anger if she wishes to get love. We do not wish those we love to desert us, for the first strong fear in life is that of desertion. The martyr's deepest fear is of being abandoned. Such a threat brings forth rage and the wish to kill, usually repressed from awareness.

These violent feelings are natural: we should allow ourselves to feel angry enough to kill someone who hurts us, since murderous feelings do not in themselves constitute a crime for which we will be punished. We do not have to pay the high psychic price of repressed anger and guilt. Or of acting like a martyr, which will never bring us the love we want, but simply more depression.

Chapter 9

WHEN DREAMS COME TRUE—A GLIMPSE AT SUCCESSFUL WOMEN

Fortunately for many women, the conflicts of their earliest years are not so intense as to interfere with their realistic desires as they achieve some of their girlhood dreams.

These women have married, borne children, and had successful careers. Or they have married and raised children, but never wanted a life outside their home, content to share their husbands' success. Still others have married but preferred not to have children. And there are women who have pursued a career, choosing not to marry or have children. All were aware of what they wanted, chose their lifestyle consciously, and spent little or no time bemoaning their decision.

The actress Rosalind Russell was one such woman. In her recent autobiography, *Life is a Banquet,* written with

Chris Chase, Miss Russell (the fourth of seven children growing up in Waterbury, Connecticut) said: "I wanted a home, a husband, children, a variety of experience. My life has been sweet, and though this may sound funny, I feel it's been fairly normal. Sound familiar? Domestic? Ordinary? Thank God it is, and has been. I caught the right guy, he knows and understands me and cares about me, and that's been my chief blessing."

She declined in 1941 to sign a second seven-year contract with Metro-Goldwyn-Mayer. She said she wanted to spend more time than such a commitment would permit with the man she married that year, Frederick Brisson, who became a successful producer, and to raising children. When she died in November of 1976, she had just observed her thirty-fifth wedding anniversary in the same house in which she had lived as a newlywed. Her only child, a son, is the deputy public administrator of Los Angeles County.

Rosalind Russell made fifty-one films in a career that stretched from 1934 to 1971. She proved it was possible for a woman to have a successful film career as well as a fulfilling home life.

Beverly Sills is another woman whose childhood dreams came true—a successful operatic career after years of work, marriage and family. She has managed to combine a happy home life and a spectacular career as few women have.

When asked about her girlhood dreams, Betty Friedan said, "I didn't have any." She explained, "I felt I had to take a leap over a void. All I knew was that I didn't want to lead a life like my mother's, though I wanted to marry and have children. I also wanted to be an actress but knew I wasn't pretty enough."

Ms. Friedan achieved quite a "leap." She married, raised children and became the leader of the women's liberation movement with her book *The Feminine Mystique* and her public speaking, in which she put her acting talents to good use.

Liv Ullman, in her autobiography *Changing,* writes evocatively of her life as a young girl, and as an actress, of her first marriage and subsequent relationship with the film director Ingmar Bergman, who fathered her daughter, Linn. In the *Epilogue,* addressed to her daughter, she says: "Through the years I have struggled with my profession. Tried to find out who I am and why I am."

Then she adds, "Your thin little body is as close to life as I have come . . . I stand and look at you and am closer to you than anything else I know about . . . You are a part of me which is completely free."

She expresses regret she has not had time to "follow" her small daughter more closely. She concludes the book, an eloquent, fragmentary portrait of her life, with these words:

"Do you understand, dear Linn—out there with the children you laugh with and the secret games you play alone, and the fragrances and the colors and all the beauty which is still your world—do you understand that I really have no valid reason not to run out to you and live your life?

"It may be the lost kingdom of childhood I am in constant search for."

That lost kingdom, in a sense, is part of every woman's search for happiness and success as she makes peace with her childhood dreams. She establishes a new kingdom, one that fulfills some childhood dreams though leaving other dreams untouched.

Asked if her dreams had been fulfilled, author Anne Edwards, whose latest book on the life of Vivien Leigh has received high acclaim, replied:

"Dreams change as do the lives of the people they

inhabit. But they are with us long enough to become part of our every day, our security. Fulfilling them often leaves a void. My dreams were fulfilled in one short summer. When it happened I felt suddenly bereft. There had been no sound of crashing cymbals. Instead there was this terrifying silence. For a week I suffered an agonizing depression. What possible justification could I have to be unhappy? After all, my dreams had been fulfilled. On the eighth day I awoke with the most marvelous quaver of anxiety. The autumn night had birthed a parcel of new dreams. They seem like the impossible but they are now my most joyous companions, with me whenever I am alone, challenging me to overtake them; a challenge I quickly and happily accepted."

In the field of law, Harriet F. Pilpel has become internationally famous, at the same time achieving her childhood dreams of marriage and children. Her rewarding career includes her law practice, pioneer work with the national and international Planned Parenthood organizations, achievements in the field of censorship and the law, and books and articles on various subjects, including the status of women. In 1977 Ms. Pilpel became the first woman in its history to be honored by the New York City Bar Association at its annual Twelfth Night celebration.

As early as the age of ten, she knew she wanted to become a lawyer. She explains: "I . . . had an uncle who was a lawyer and he and my aunt seemed to be having the best time of my many relatives. They traveled all over the world. They apparently had more money to spend than anyone else in the family. Their apartment was decorated in elegant style. My aunt always had gorgeous clothes, some of which were handed down to me. I attributed all this to the fact my uncle was a lawyer."

She enjoyed public speaking and debating in high

school and college. She says the best reason for adhering to her choice of law as she grew older was that "I always have been a liberal, interested in social change and I believed lawyers better able than others to help effect the needed changes."

Ms. Pilpel praises her mother (one of sixteen children) and father for not putting obstacles in her path to self-realization. She says, "I grew up in a very favorable environment in which it was assumed that all three daughters were not just going to get married and have children, but also would enjoy careers—as each of us has." She adds, "My husband was also encouraging—since his mother's sisters were all 'career women' I don't think it occurred to him I'd be anything else. And he was always ready to share household responsibilities."

In the process of achieving her goals, she recalls, "I, like so many other women, was in a fairly constant state of conflict. When I was low, I felt I was not doing right by my husband, my children, or my career. And that by trying to do all three, I wasn't doing any one well. I kept apologizing to my children, particularly. They kept reassuring me they felt I was 'a good mother.' Now that they're grown up and successes in their own right, their recollections are not that I was a bad mother but that I bored them to death by my constant apologizing and need for reassurance."

At times, Ms. Pilpel says, her conflict over home versus career was so intense she sought the help of a psychiatrist. Eventually, she said, "I learned I did not have to be a 100 percent wife, 100 percent mother, and 100 percent lawyer. It was extremely helpful when the psychiatrist asked, 'Don't you think maybe that by doing all three, each may be enriching the others?' "

She has since noted, she comments, when women of drive and ambition do not continue, at least in part, an independent career life outside the home, "they seem to be less good mothers and wives than when they do. Such women, when they look to their families for all their satisfactions, almost inevitably will be disappointed and frustrated." She adds she is convinced many women of her mother's generation wanted both home and career though society did not then give most of them the option of "being a person outside as well as inside the home."

Author Flora Rheta Schreiber also knew from the start what she wanted and headed for it. Her powerful book *Sybil* sold millions of copies all over the world and became one of 1976's outstanding television features. She says that, for the most part, her deepest wishes as a girl have come true: "As a small girl I dreamed I was going to be famous as a writer. I wrote, at the age of thirteen, on graduation from elementary school, that my ambition was to be 'author and teacher' and today I am both." (She is Professor of English and Speech at John Jay College of Criminal Justice of the City University of New York, where she is also Assistant to the President and Director of Public Relations and Publications.)

Did Professor Schreiber ever dream of Prince Charming? "I wanted a Prince Charming and fell in love with him on two different occasions. But I didn't want to marry either prince," she says. "I wanted romantic love but I didn't want the dailyness and mundanity of marriage."

Her parents had "a beautiful marriage," she recalls, but she decided early in life she did not want to be a housewife. She rigidly resisted learning to cook, telling her mother, "If I were a boy, I wouldn't mind learning to cook and keep house, but as a girl, I can't risk being cast in the role of housekeeper. It would be an unbearable bore and destroy my real aspirations." Her mother replied sympathetically, "This is your decision. You have to act according to your personality, your individual wishes. Don't ever come near the kitchen." And, says Professor Schreiber, "I never did!"

She comments, "My mother treated me with infinite respect, honoring me for establishing my priorities early and for making those priorities work. My imaginative, cultivated, understanding parents (my erudite, Phi Beta Kappa father as well) went along with me, the admired, only child. My standards became their standards for me. Or were my standards really a synthesis of theirs? At any rate, I am deeply grateful to them for twice making me —not only through nature but also through nurture. They gave me an unconditional love I shall always remember."

Lillian Hellman achieved the most wished-for of her childhood dreams, as she describes them in her book *Pentimento*. While still a young girl she kept a "writer's book," which she described as "a collection of mishmash, the youthful beginnings of a girl who hoped to write."

She married writer Arthur Kober ("a pleasant marriage that was not to last"), then had a long-time relationship with the writer Dashiell Hammett, which she said "survived for the best of all reasons, the pleasure of each other."

"All my life I believed in the changes I could, and sometimes did, make in a nature I so often didn't like, but now it seems to me that time made alterations and mutations rather than true reforms; and so I am left with so much of the past that I have no right to think it very different from the present," she says.

Her awareness of inner conflicts is perceptively and dramatically shown in her plays and books. She writes, "It is possible to feel many conflicts and not know they are conflicts when you are young . . ." And:

"(God help all children as they move into a time of life they do not understand and must struggle through with precepts they have picked from the garbage cans of older people, clinging with the passion of the lost to odds and ends that will mess them up for all time, or hating the trash so much they will waste their future on the hatred.)"

Many women who have achieved success accept that life holds pain as well as pleasure. A number have sought therapy in order to understand this and other psychic truths. Patty Duke, the actress, was one. She achieved her childhood dream of marrying, doing so at eighteen, but the marriage "was a disaster." Therapy helped her become aware she was "emotionally unequipped to take care of a man," she says.

As a result of psychoanalysis, she realized her obsessive "drive to succeed" had kept her from living happily with herself and others. She no longer needs "the love of everybody," she asserts, to make up for the illusory love she had always sought in vain.

Margie Hart, once the nation's leading stripteaser, discovered that success and the admiration of her body by millions did not lessen her self-hatred. She went into analysis, afterward declaring, "I don't hate Margie Hart any more."

Jayne Meadows, now married to comedian Steve Allen, was another actress who propelled herself into an unhappy early marriage, after which she suffered many psychosomatic illnesses and depression. She achieved her girlhood dream of becoming an actress but realized she was only "escaping into the highly neurotic world of show-business where I hoped to become famous and loved by everybody." It brought no happiness.

She found a "brilliant and sensitive" psychiatrist who, she said, "gave me the courage and strength to break the unusually strong, neurotic ties with my family and to see that it was possible for me to really love my parents in a healthy way. For the first time I was able to see them as human beings with human weaknesses and not as the all-powerful authority figures which had so frightened me in the past."

Though she was afraid of becoming a mother, woke many nights "screaming from nightmares about childbirth," she decided to have a baby. As a result of therapy, she welcomed the responsibility of becoming a parent, able to accept her duties as wife and mother and her career as an actress.

Vivian Vance, known to America's television viewers from the "I Love Lucy" series and "The Lucy Show", says that for years she played comedienne onstage but her life offstage was anything but amusing. She felt deeply depressed without knowing why. Even as she headed for stardom, wanting to please everyone along the way, she felt there was "another, more genuine kind of life I was missing."

She became physically and emotionally ill, suffering arthritis and other ailments. When she went into therapy all her physical symptoms vanished immediately. She was able to divorce a man with whom she had been unhappy and to make a satisfying second marriage. "When you marry neurotically," she explains, "you marry someone like your parents, wanting his approval, just as you wanted the approval of your parents. You are constantly living for someone else's actions and reactions, rather than living out your own life."

Today, Ms. Vance says, "The neurosis doesn't rule me any more." Her therapy enabled her to "wake up every morning and face the day with joy, knowing that you're going to do the best you can, instead of allowing life to stampede you. You accept the day with its joys and sorrows, instead of feeling depressed and despairing.

You care only about your own approval, not that of others."

Actress Janice Rule, who has become a therapist, reports that as a result of her personal analysis, she does not feel, as many artists and actors fear, she was "divested of creative imagination or emotional power." "On the contrary," she says, "these forces are stronger in my work; they are freer and contain more understanding of human complexity. Self-esteem, based more internally than externally, and growing faith in my own perceptions, have lessened the chances of undue influence by untalented directors, hostile fellow actors, or destructive acting teachers."

Ms. Rule, married to actor Ben Gazzara, makes the point an actor's past can be valuable in the creation of a role onstage, but that without insight the conflicts of his past may propel the performer "into a great deal of painful reality."

She cites as example a fantasy she herself used as a young actress to help her characterization when she played the role of an adolescent whose father had run away years before the action of the play began. No clue was given by the playwright as to the father's character. Ms. Rule fantasied the father as the only person in the girl's life who took her seriously, talked to her, taught her about the world, treated her as a person. Years later, after therapy, she realized she imagined a dream father very different from her own and had become so submerged in this fantasy father-daughter relationship that shortly before the play closed, she became involved with a fatherly man and married him even though she had misgivings about the marriage. It lasted only two months.

"This is not say that my father problem would't have driven me to act out in real life, without my preoccupation with the fantasied father in the play," she explains.

"However, I personally doubt that I would have gone to such lengths as to undertake a marriage. Eighteen months of living with a dream father left me with a hunger for such an experience in real life."

Ms. Rule points out that the actress who is well aware of her inner conflicts does not become caught up in the fantasies of the roles she plays. She is able to separate her own conflicts from those of the onstage character without, however, losing the artistic ability to identify with that character. Such an actress, as Ms. Rule puts it, "uses both her reasonable, observing, analyzing self, and her irrational, subjective experiencing self."

Of her girlhood dreams, Judianne Densen-Gerber, president of Odyssey Institute, Inc., which helps emotionally troubled young people, says: "My odyssey in living, in many ways, has far exceeded both my past and present dreams. It is exciting, rewarding and deeply gratifying to know I make a difference not only in saving individual lives, but in changing social attitudes in such areas as child pornography. No one could fantasize the joy of watching a young woman, formerly a prostitute and addict, move from rejecting her failure-to-thrive baby, to being a happy individual who sings while cuddling her healthy baby."

Many women like Ms. Densen-Gerber, are today fighting some of society's most important battles, as well as understanding their own inner conflicts. The sad truth is, however, that for countless other women, the fantasy in their lives has become more powerful than reality. These are the women whose conscious dreams of marriage, children, and career never come true because girlhood fantasies, revolving around sexual and aggressive conflicts that should have lost their ability to influence thinking and behavior, are still strong enough to block self-fulfillment.

Chapter 10

HOW TO MAKE YOUR FANTASIES WORK FOR YOU

Many women are in touch with their feelings. They know what they want, whether it be career or marriage, or both. They are content with their choices and go through life with a serenity that reflects coming to terms with childhood conflicts.

Inner serenity is not to be mistaken for a feeling of dead calm or dullness. Some women fear if they face their deeper feelings they will lose the intensity that has driven them into creativity and success. Quite the opposite is true: self-awareness removes the conflicts that obsessively propel a woman into hyperactivity or into creativity accompanied by a high degree of anxiety. When a woman denies hidden conflicts, she may create as though in the midst of a perpetual storm of anxiety. Or she may withdraw to an almost catatonic state. Self-awareness enhances the creative drive and the ability to think clearly as the anxiety underlying the driven feeling subsides. Anxiety is comprised of repressed angry and sexual urges and fantasies revolving about them.

Inner serenity comes from acknowledging oneself as human in the fullest sense of the word—not only able to feel good, thoughtful, compassionate, and constructive, but also evil, selfish, merciless, and destructive. As Robert Louis Stevenson expressed it, "We all have feelings that would shame hell."

To be human means hating at times. Feeling the impulse to steal, to kill, to maim, to destroy someone in cannibalistic fantasy. Feeling torn by jealousy. Wishing to be taken care of like a baby when the going gets difficult. Feeling terror-stricken. Wanting to express the sexual and aggressive urge on all levels—oral, anal, and phallic—in times of stress. Wishing to masturbate to relieve tension. Perhaps wishing occasionally to have sexual intimacy with a partner of one's own sex. Or more than one partner at a time.

There is no emotion, no fantasy, a woman does not share with every other woman on earth. It is only in the particulars of her experiences that she differs from the next woman—the events of her life make her unique.

Fantasies remain active, causing distress to a woman, if she has had to use them excessively to defend against the hatred in her life. The amount of hatred a little girl feels toward her parents is the chief difficulty of her early life, causing her conflicts. Hatred, when it is excessive, stems from feeling unloved, unwanted. It is not always caused by the acts of physically brutal parents. Hatred may fill the heart of a little girl whose parents give her the feeling they wish she had never been born. Or that she had been born a boy. Or who openly favor a brother or sister. Children respond naturally to hatred with hatred.

Many women, as little girls, had to quickly hide, from themselves and others, normal feelings of hatred, jealousy, selfishness. They were never permitted to be in touch with what they truly felt. They grew up denying what to them were "wicked," "shameful," and "embarrassing" emotions and wishes. They have never realized that the wish is not the same as the deed and that they need not feel guilty at what they consider dangerous wishes. They remain caught in conflicts carried with them from childhood—conflicts that center on "good" versus "bad." It is "bad" to show sexual desire for a father, "good" to deny sensuous feelings. It is "bad" to talk back to a mother, "good" to be sweet, polite, and obedient. It is "bad" to hit a smaller brother or sister, "good" to take care of them. It is "bad" to touch one's own body to create a pleasurable feeling, "good" to deny all wishes for sexual pleasure. It is "bad" to admit feelings of wanting to be taken care of like a baby, "good" to appear totally self-reliant.

The little girl whose parents understand her conflicts can cope with her opposing feelings—her wish to be "bad" versus her wish to be "good." The little girl whose parents often treat her as though they wish she were out of their lives, who do not consider her a person in her own right, will suffer as an adult from hateful and vengeful fantasies.

What *do* women want? Most say they want the conventional things—love, marriage, children, the right to work at whatever interests them. These are *reasonable* goals, goals approved by society. But women's fantasies show they also want *unreasonable* things—to marry their fathers, to have their fathers' babies, to feel excessively dependent, to be men, or to kill members of their families. Such "unconscionable" wishes clash with the civilized behavior established by parents and society at large.

A psychic deadlock may ensue, thwarting or paralyzing a woman's thought or action.

A number of women live more in the world of fantasy than in the real world. The world of fantasy is comprised of what Freud called "psychic reality." It is made up of our infantile, frustrated wishes. They are inappropriate to reality—unfortunately, however, that does not mean they remain psychically quiescent.

The danger lies in the fact that the wishes inherent in our fantasies may exert a more powerful influence on us than the reasonable wishes appropriate to reality. Thus, the answer to Freud's question is that in many instances women want the fulfillment of wishes stemming from powerful childhood fantasies. These fantasies control their real-life behavior and make it impossible for them to achieve the more appropriate, conventional goals they publicly claim to want.

In other words, the psychic reality of many a woman, made up of primitive childhood wishes, may determine her acts even though she is unaware of it and believes she possesses "free will." If she lives driven by "psychic reality" she does *not* have free choice: she is controlled by her deeper wishes, inappropriate to reality, which would, if carried out, disgrace and condemn her in her own and in society's eyes. She would lose all self-esteem if the hidden wishes were fulfilled.

Most women repress their childhood wishes except as they escape in disguised form in dreams. It is far healthier from an emotional point of view, if a woman feels very troubled, to face these hidden wishes rather than to keep denying them, since there is no way of coping with a fantasy that is unconscious. When wishes considered to be taboo remain unconscious, they perpetuate the patterns that lead inevitably to self-destructive behavior and unfulfilled lives.

What are some of the destructive patterns into which unconscious wishes may drive a woman? The following indicate attitudes or characterlogical symptoms behind which lie fantasies (behind which lie the specific experiences of a woman's life that contribute to the molding of her personality):

1.   If she still waits for Prince Charming, insisting she wants to get married but never finding an appropriate man or always choosing one who is irresponsible or emotionally unstable in some way.

2.   If she is overly possessive, consumed with jealousy each time her husband or lover looks at another woman.

3.   If she must always be in control, never able to consider the wishes of others.

4.   If she usually seeks someone else to take responsibility for her decisions, unable to make up her own mind.

5.   If she allows a man to be overly possessive with her, virtually becoming his slave.

6.   If she feels she must be "perfect" and demands that others be.

7.   If she is so depressed she cannot work or function in any respect for days at a time.

8.   If the only way she can relate to others is through anger.

9.   If she cannot remain sexually faithful to one man.

10.   If she envies men, showing contempt for them, and competes angrily with them.

11.   If she is always changing jobs, never content with one field of work.

12.   If she works excessively, unable to take time for pleasure.

13.   If she dresses carelessly, does not pay attention to her personal appearance, is unclean in regard to her body.

14.   If she has a phobia that terrifies her, such as fear of crowds, of high places, or of flying.

15.   If she cannot cry when it is appropriate—when someone she loves dies or when she feels deeply hurt.

16.   If she cannot tolerate being alone, always hurling herself into activity.

17.   If, when she is with someone, she must talk incessantly, unable to bear mutual silences.

18.   If she gambles excessively, unable to give up the addiction.

19.   If she is always in debt, living over her head financially.

20.   If she is miserly, afraid to spend money for her own pleasure or that of friends.

21.   If she drinks excessively, losing days of work or other activity because of it.

22.   If she is overweight and unable to diet even for reasons of health.

23.   If she cannot give up cigarettes though her doctor has told her they are dangerous to her health.

24.   If her conversation consists of complaint after complaint and she is unable to be concerned about the troubles of friends, lost as she is in her own misery.

25.   If she is so sexually attracted to other women that she is unable to desire a man.

26.   If masturbation is her only or chief form of sexual outlet.

27.   If she needs a man to beat her, psychologically or physically, before she can become sexually aroused.

28.   If she is afraid of success and cannot compete with her peers.

29.   If she is always envious of anyone else's success, even that of a dear friend.

30.   If she considers life a "game," not taking seriously anything that happens to her, even though it may be very important.

31.   If her life is one seeming crisis after another, caused by her over-reaction to trivial events.

32.   If she continually screams at her children for minor acts of misbehavior, expecting perfection from them.

33.   If she allows her children to do anything they wish without providing guidelines or controls.

34.   If she can never allow someone else to do something nice for her, too afraid to receive.

35.   If she believes herself a martyr, taken advantage of by everyone.

36.   If she is always criticizing, rarely saying an approving or loving word about anyone.

If a woman finds herself a victim of any of the above patterns, she would do well to try to become aware of the fantasies, wishes, and conflicts that underlie those patterns. Otherwise, the patterns will perpetuate themselves ceaselessly and she will always feel an underlying unhappiness. Many of the fantasies causing these destructive patterns have been described in detail in the previous chapters.

To resolve a conflict, it is not enough to be intellectually aware of it. We must also emotionally experience what we feel in connection with the conflict. We must *feel* the rage, the fear, the jealousy, the desire for revenge. If this proves too difficult, a woman may have to seek help from a therapist in order to live through the repressed feelings.

One woman of forty-five was unable to cry before she

entered psychoanalysis. Her trust in the analyst eventually permitted her to shed tears and to get angry. Both she and the analyst were delighted one day when she was able to say, after he had kept her waiting ten minutes while seeing another patient, "You're a bastard!"

Our fantasies and feelings go on in our minds and bodies even as we breathe. The issue is whether they are so powerful that they determine what we do or whether we are emotionally strong enough to consciously mould our lives. We can make our fantasies work for us once we become aware of them.

If a woman realizes she is repeating over and over the pattern of seeking men she wants to "save" from their destructive ways—the so-called rescue fantasy—she can use this wish more constructively if she accepts it as reflecting her own childhood wish to be "saved" from what she believed cruel and neglectful parents. She can seek work as a nurse, social worker or other member of the helping professions, thus "saving" in a more realistic way. She will also be able to choose a man who has "saved" himself, a far more suitable choice because of his greater independence.

Or, if a woman is careless and sloppy about her appearance, she can realize she is carrying out her fantasy of rebellion against a mother who perhaps forced her too early, or too angrily, to be toilet trained. The woman might then use her desire to be "messy" in an artistic way, with paints and palette. Or start a flea market or thrift shop, where chaos reigns and articles are piled high in all directions.

To bring a buried conflict to awareness means freeing oneself of guilt. As Freud discovered, the repressed memories associated to a guilty feeling cause unhappiness. The guilt stems from the conflict over two opposing wishes. One wish is to carry out a pleasurable act based on a sexual or aggressive impulse. The other wish is not to carry out the act because it is taboo, going against a parent's and society's decrees. As the conflict is brought to awareness, so too the realization that it belonged to childhood, not to the present. And the guilt disappears.

Civilization is built on the sublimation of our tabooed wishes—on a certain amount of guilt, if you will. We all sublimate to a certain degree, unless we are so emotionally ill that we become schizophrenic or carry out violent impulses. If we recognize our fantasies and conflicts, we can *choose* our sublimation, not be driven to it by obsessional feelings that prevent our ever fully enjoying what we do. When an act or thought is obsessional, it contains guilt. Precious psychic energy is expended to keep the underlying wish and fantasy buried from awareness. This energy is freed for constructive use when the repressed wish is made conscious.

For instance, if a woman becomes aware of her girlhood wish to have a baby by her father and realizes this was a natural, normal wish at the time and one about which she need never feel guilty, she will enjoy sex far more on the emotional level, able to look at a man in his own right, not as a projected father image.

A woman who knows her hidden fantasies will enjoy sublimation, not rebel against it. She will put to lie Pope's lines:

> The ruling passion, be it what it will,
> The ruling passion conquers reason still.

We all tend to hide deeper fantasies from awareness for one simple reason—they are painful. Our hidden fantasies are never palatable or pleasurable to the adult self. But we suffer a greater pain if our lives are ruled by unknown wishes. Once we bring to conscious thought our secret fantasies, we expose to the light of reason childhood impulses and conflicts that may have been causing us to act in a harmful way to ourselves and others. As Freud said, "The voice of the intellect is a soft one but it does not rest until it has gained a hearing."

Part of growing up emotionally is the ability to face and handle mixed feelings of love and hate. As we can do this, we realize we do not have to act out of childhood feelings once appropriate between ourselves and our parents but no longer suitable for an adult relationship. We are able to look at ourselves with a certain amount of objectivity, to take into account the feelings of others. We do not need to blame someone else for feelings within ourselves which we consider terrifying or shameful.

As we come to know our fantasies, we can love more fully—give love, accept love, and share love. Our tender feelings will come to the fore as we become aware of our fury. We no longer have to use or abuse sex as an outlet for hate but can enjoy it as part of love. We will possess more self-esteem, respecting ourselves and others—not idolizing others, as we once did our parents, but feeling a new respect founded on affection and trust. We will take joy in our achievements and those of others.

We make peace, in a very real sense, with the prehistoric part of ourselves, one that caused torment stemming not from reality but from inner conflicts.

To know our fantasies is to embark on a rewarding inner journey. Many women do not, or cannot, take the time and trouble to look at their lives, unaware of the advice of Socrates: "The life which is unexamined is not worth living."

If a woman knows her deepest wishes and does not deny what she feels, she can accept that life holds pain as well as pleasure, frustration as well as fulfillment, loss as well as gain. She forgives herself for possessing what she once believed savage, wicked wishes, now to her an understandable part of being a child.

She will, in the words of Dr. Jerome L. Singer, "move differently through the world." She will be able to "savor her emotions" and "experience greater control over them, as well as a greater capacity to express them." She will get acquainted with feelings never before accessible. She will, according to Singer, exert "a heightened capacity" for examining her wishes and plans in relation to a variety of alternative possibilities and options.

Beauty, wealth, and fame do not compensate a woman for the failure to know herself. It is sad to realize that Greta Garbo, who had what we think of as "everything," interviewed recently at the age of seventy-two, believes she has "messed up" her life.

The actress spends two months each summer in Klosters, a Swiss ski resort, living in a small apartment. There she reads, sleeps, and waits, "I really don't know for what," she confesses. "I'm restless everywhere and unable to settle down. I think I always have been." She adds, "If only I knew where to go."

Most of the year Garbo lives in her apartment on fashionable Beekman Place in Manhattan. Photographers have snapped her striding along the street, wearing tinted glasses. She takes long, solitary walks, even in the rain. "These walks," she declares, "are just an escape. When I go walking alone, I think back over my life and the past. I am not happy with the way I made my life."

The woman who once said, "I want to be alone," seems to have achieved her wish but is still unhappy. There are many other successful women caught in the same anguish of inner conflicts of which they were never aware, conflicts that have made them feel their lives are "messed up."

Freud saw life as a struggle between "pleasure" and "unpleasure." The pleasurable feelings, stemming from childhood, include the wish to have sex whenever we want with whomever we want, or to kill anyone who hurts us or interferes with our desires. The frustration of these infantile wishes causes unpleasure, or psychic pain.

But there is another kind of pleasure that comes in knowing the truth about ourselves. Each moment of insight about the repressed self brings a reward, a sense of inner glow to mind and body. The more insights, the more serenity, and the deeper the feeling we call happiness.

And, the more insights, the less the need to depend on the fantasies of childhood for a wished-for happiness that can never be. Using fantasy, instead, for imaginative, creative living raises fantasy to its highest art.

Once a woman is aware of her infantile fantasies, and frees herself from the guilt attached to them, she has free choice—true emotional liberation.

SELECTED BIBLIOGRAPHY

CHAPTER 1

Friedman, Lawrence. *How Much Pleasure? How Much Pain?* Van Nuys, California: Barlo Press, 1971.

Mitchell, Juliet. *Psychoanalysis and Feminism.* New York: Vintage Books, 1975.

Singer, Jerome. "Imagery Formation and Use in Various Psychotherapies." Paper delivered at the annual meeting of the American Psychiatric Association, May 1976, at Miami Beach, Fla.

———. *How Women See Their Roles: A Change in Attitudes.* Bethesda, Maryland: Publication of the Division of Extramural Research Programs, National Institute of Mental Health, 1976.

CHAPTER 2

Arlow, Jacob A. "Unconscious Fantasy and Disturbances of Conscious Experiences." A. A. Brill Lecture, New York Academy of Medicine, March 1964.

Bak, Robert C. "Being in Love and Object Loss." *International Journal of Psychoanalysis.* Vol. 54, 1973.

Barchilon, Jacques. "Beauty and the Beast: From Myth to Fairy Tale." *The Psychoanalytic Review.* Vol. 46, 1959.

Devereux, George. "Laws to Live By—Not Under." *Community Education,* Vol. 1, 1965. George Junior Republic Association, Inc.

Eidelberg, Ludwig. "In Pursuit of Happiness." *The Psychoanalytic Review.* Vol. 38, 1951.

Freud, Sigmund. *Formulations on the Two Principles of Mental Functioning.* Standard Edition, Vol. 3. London: The Hogarth Press, 1962.

――――. *Introductory Lectures on Psycho-Analysis.* Standard Edition, Vol. 12. London: The Hogarth Press, 1958.

――――. *On the Sexual Theories of Children. Collected Papers,* Vol. II. London: The Hogarth Press, 1953.

Gray, Francine du Plessix. *Lovers and Tyrants.* New York: Simon & Schuster, 1976.

Grotjahn, Martin. *Beyond Laughter.* New York: McGraw-Hill, 1957.

Katz, Leo. "The Rumpelstiltskin Complex." *Contemporary Psychoanalysis.* Vol. 10:1, 1974.

Lorand, Sandor. "Fairy Tales and Neurosis." *The Psychoanalytic Quarterly.* Vol. IV, 1935.

Mintz, Thomas. "The Meaning of the Rose in Beauty and the Beast." *The Psychoanalytic Review.* Vol. 56, 1969.

Rado, Sandor. *Adaptational Psychodynamics: Motivation and Control.* New York: Science House, 1969. Edited by Dr. Jean Jameson and Dr. Henriette Klein.

Ricklin, Franz. "Wishfulfillment and Fairy Tales." *Nervous and Mental Disease Monographs.* 1915.

Róheim, Géza. "Psycho-Analysis and the Folk-Tale." *International Journal of Psychoanalysis.* Vol. III, 1922.

Rubenstein, Ben. "The Meaning of the Cinderella Story in the Development of a Little Girl." *American Imago.* Vol. 12, 1955.

Schwartz, Emanuel K. "A Psychoanalytic Study of the Fairy Tale." *American Journal of Psychotherapy.* Vol. X, 1956.

CHAPTER 3

Deutsch, Helene. *The Psychology of Women.* New York: Grune & Stratton, 1944.

Hite, Shere. *The Hite Report.* New York: Macmillan, 1976.

Jones, Ernest. "The Early Development of Female Sexuality." *International Journal of Psychoanalysis.* Vol. VIII, 1927.

Lee, Patrick C., and Stewart, Robert Sussman (eds.). *Sex Differences, Cultural and Developmental Dimensions.* New York: Urizen Books, 1976.

Rado, Sandor. *Adaptational Psychodynamics: Motivation and Control.* New York: Science House, 1969. Edited by Dr. Jean Jameson and Dr. Henriette Klein.

CHAPTER 4

Abraham, Karl. "Manifestations of the Female Castration Complex." *International Journal of Psychoanalysis.* Vol. III, 1922.

Bonaparte, Marie. *Female Sexuality.* New York: International Universities Press, 1953.

Fenichel, Otto. "The Symbolic Equation: Girl = Phallus." *Collected Papers of Otto Fenichel.* Second Series. New York: W. W. Norton, 1954.

Freud, Sigmund. "Concerning the Sexuality of Women." *The Psychoanalytic Quarterly.* Vol. I, 1932.

———. *Femininity.* The Complete Introductory Lectures on Psychoanalysis. New York: W. W. Norton, 1966.

———. *Three Essays on the Theory of Sexuality.* London: Imago Publishing Co., Ltd., 1949.

Gadpaille, Warren. *The Cycles of Sex.* New York: Charles Scribner's Sons, 1975.

Greenacre, Phyllis. "Penis Awe and Its Relation to Penis Envy." Chapter in *Emotional Growth* by Dr. Phyllis Greenacre. New York: International Universities Press, 1971.

———. "Special Problems of Early Female Sexual Development." *The Psychoanalytic Study of the Child,* Vol. V. New York: International Universities Press, 1950.

Horney, Karen. "The Dread of Women." *International Journal of Psychoanalysis.* Vol. VIII, 1932.

Lewin, Bertram. "The Body as Phallus." *The Psychoanalytic Quarterly.* Vol. 2, 1933.

Lorand, Rhoda L. *Love, Sex and the Teenager.* New York: Macmillan, 1965.

Riviere, Joan. "Womanliness as a Masquerade." *International Journal of Psychoanalysis.* Vol. X, 1929.

CHAPTER 5

Bonaparte, Marie. *Female Sexuality.* New York: International Universities Press, 1953.

Delaney, Janice, Lupton, Mary Jane, and Toth, Emily. *The Curse: A Cultural History of Menstruation.* New York: E. P. Dutton, 1976.

Freud, Sigmund. *A Child is Being Beaten. Collected Papers.* Vol. II.

———. *The Interpretation of Dreams.* New York: Basic Books, 1970.

Grotjahn, Martin. "The Changing View of Sexual Pathology." *Contemporary Psychoanalysis.* Vol. IX, 1974.

Stewart, Walter A. *Psychoanalysis: The First Ten Years.* New York: Macmillan, 1967.

———. *The Secret of Dreams.* New York: Macmillan, 1972.

Stone, Leo. "On the Principal Obscene Word in the English Language." *International Journal of Psychoanalysis.* Vol. XXXV, 1954.

Tanay, Emanuel, and Freeman, Lucy. *The Murderers.* Indianapolis/New York: Bobbs-Merrill, 1977.

CHAPTER 6

Deutsch, Helene. *The Psychology of Women.* New York: Grune & Stratton, 1944.

Horney, Karen. *Feminine Psychology.* New York: W. W. Norton, 1967.

Rheingold, Joseph. *The Fear of Being a Woman.* New York: Grune & Stratton, 1964.

Spotnitz, Hyman, and Freeman, Lucy. *How to Be Happy Though Pregnant.* New York: Coward, McCann and Geoghegan, 1969.

CHAPTER 7

Abraham, Karl. *The Psychological Relation Between Sexuality and Alcoholism. Selected Papers.* New York: Basic Books, 1953.

Benedek, Therese. "Dominant Ideas and Their Relation to Morbid Cravings." *International Journal of Psychoanalysis.* Vol. XVII, 1936.

Bergler, Edmund. *The Psychology of Gambling.* New York: Hill & Wang, 1957.

Bychowski, Gustav. "On Neurotic Obesity." *The Psychoanalytic Review.* Vol. XXXVII, 1950.

Glover, Edward. "On the Aetiology of Drug Addiction." *International Journal of Psychoanalysis.* Vol. XIII, 1932.

Kohut, Heinz, *The Analysis of the Self.* New York: International Universities Press, 1971.

Lindner, Robert. *The Fifty-Minute Hour.* New York: Rinehart & Co., 1954.

Rochlin, Gregory. *Griefs and Discontents.* Boston: Little, Brown & Co., 1965.

CHAPTER 8

Abraham, Karl. *Notes on the Psychoanalytical Investigation and Treatment of Manic-Depressive Insanity and Allied Conditions. Selected Papers.* New York: Basic Books, 1953.

Freud, Anna. *The Psycho-analytical Treatment of Children.* London: Imago Publishing Co., Ltd., 1946.

Freud, Sigmund. *The Economic Problem in Masochism. Collected Papers,* Vol. II.

————. *Mourning and Melancholia.* Standard Edition, Vol. 14, 1957.

Gralnick, Alexander. "The Carrington Family: A Psychiatric and Social Study Illustrating the Psychosis of Association or Folie à Deux." *The Psychiatric Quarterly.* Vol. XVIII, 1943.

Greenacre, Phyllis. "Perversions, General Consideration Regarding Their Genetic and Dynamic Background." *The Psychoanalytic Study of the Child,* Vol. XXIII. New York: International Universities Press, 1968.

Jacobson, Edith. "The Effect of Disappointment on Ego and Super-Ego Formation in Normal and Depressive Development." *The Psychoanalytic Review.* Vol. 33, 1946.

Klein, Melanie. *The Psychoanalysis of Children.* New York: Grove Press, 1960.

Lorand, Sandor. *Dynamics and Therapy of Depressive States. The Psychoanalytic Review.* Vol. 24, 1937.

Mahler, Margaret. "On the Significance of the Normal Separation-Individuation Phase." Chapter in *Drives, Affects, Behavior,* Vol. 2, edited by Max Schur. New York: International Universities Press, 1966.

Rado, Sandor. "The Problem of Melancholia." *International Journal of Psychoanalysis.* Vol. XIX, 1928.

CHAPTER 9

Freeman, Lucy (ed.). *Celebrities on the Couch.* Los Angeles: Price, Stern, Sloan and Ravenna Books, 1970.

Hellman, Lillian. *Pentimento.* Boston: Little, Brown & Co., 1973.

Rule, Janice. "The Actor's Identity Crises (Postanalytic Reflections of an Actress)." *International Journal of Psychoanalytic Psychotherapy.* Vol. 2, 1973.

Russell, Rosalind, and Chase, Chris. *Life is a Banquet.* New York: Random House, 1977.

Ullman, Liv. *Changing.* New York: Alfred A. Knopf, 1977.

INDEX

Abortion, 117
  fantasies of, 122-123
Abraham, Dr. Karl, 63, 66, 67-68,
  89-90, 132, 138
Adolescence and masturbation,
  55-56, 57
African tribes, sexual surgery in,
  16
After the Fall (Miller), 77
Aggressive drives
  and fairy tales, 25, 26
  and "group sex," 54
  See also Anger; Murder, Vio-
    lence
Aging
  adjusting to, 127, 148
  See also Narcissism
Alcohol, and narcissism, 137-138
Amazons, 69, 78
America, clitoral surgery in, 16
American Humane Association,
  98
Ancient man, and fantasy, 20-21
Anger
  and charm, 94, 95
  and depression, 97, 153
  and dreams, 108-109
  and fear of punishment, 105
  and feminity, 89
  and frustrated Oedipal con-
    flict, 60
  and laughter, 94

and marriage, 32
and menstruation, 107-108
and overeating, 132-133
and overprotectiveness, 106
and penis envy, 68
and phobias, 107
and sexual frustration, 47
Animism, 147
Anorexia, 137
Anxiety
  composition of, 171
  and fantasy, 20
Aquinas, St. Thomas, 69
Arapesh, 100
Artistic creations, and aggressive drives, 99
Asian tribes, sexual surgery in, 16

Bak, Dr. Robert C., 34-35
Balint, Dr. Michael, 137
Berchilon, Dr. Jacques, 27-28
Beauty and the Beast, symbolism
  of, 27-28
Benedek, Dr. Therese, 132
Bergler, Dr. Edmund, 141
Berkowitz, David, 102-103
Bisexuality, 43, 72
Bonaparte, Marie, 15, 54, 72-73
Borden Lizzie, 101-102
Boys
  and Oedipus complex, 87
  See also Men
Breasts, as phallic symbols,
  76-77
Breast feeding, 46
Brisson, Frederick, 160
Bychowski, Dr. Gustav, 133

Cannibalism, 134

189